D1228869

NATIONALISM IN BRAZIL

Nationalism in Brazil

A HISTORICAL SURVEY

E. Bradford Burns

FREDERICK A. PRAEGER, *Publishers*

New York · Washington · London

FREDERICK A. PRAEGER, PUBLISHERS
111 Fourth Avenue, New York, N.Y. 10003, U.S.A.
5, Cromwell Place, London S.W.7, England

Published in the United States of America in 1968
by Frederick A. Praeger, Inc., Publishers

© 1968 by Frederick A. Praeger, Inc.

Library of Congress Catalog Card Number: 68–20985

Printed in the United States of America

To
KAREN

Acknowledgments

I am grateful to a number of people and institutions whose generous aid made this book possible. Professor Samuel Baily awakened my interest in the subject of nationalism in Latin America. His suggestions and encouragement are appreciated. I wish to thank the following Brazilians, who kindly shared with me their ideas about nationalism in their country: Ambassador Maurício Nabuco, Professor José Honório Rodrigues, Senhor Mário da Silva Brito, Senhor Francisco de Assis Barbosa, Governor Barbosa Lima Sobrinho, Professor Alceu Amoroso Lima, Professor Cândido Mendes de Almeida, and Professor Vamireh Chacón. I am also indebted to Professor Eulália Lobo and her advanced class in Brazilian history at the Universidade do Brasil for listening to those ideas concerning the periodization of the history of nationalism in their country and for discussing them with me. In the United States, I want to thank Professors Robert N. Burr and Earl T. Glauert for their suggestions and advice. I am especially grateful to Fredrick Holden Hall of the Newberry Library for his careful reading of the manuscript and his suggestions. The Ford Foundation, through the Latin American Center of the University of California, Los Angeles, kindly provided the funds for field research in Brazil during the summer of 1965, and a fellowship from the Rockefeller Foundation made possible research and travel in 1966–67. Some of the ideas in this book were first presented in a paper, "The Development of Brazilian Nationalism," delivered at the American Historical Association meeting in San Francisco,

December 28, 1965. The opinions expressed in this book are entirely my own and do not necessarily reflect the endorsement of any of my informants. I assume full responsibility for the statements, opinions, and any errors contained herein.

E. Bradford Burns

Muscatine, Iowa
June, 1968

Contents

Acknowledgments   vii

1 The Brazilian Concept of Nationalism   3

2 The Formation of Brazil and the Cult of Nativism   12

3 The Defensive Nationalism of the Nineteenth Century   29

4 The New Brazil and the Foundations of
   Twentieth-Century Nationalism   51

5 Getúlio Vargas and Economic Nationalism   72

6 Action and Reaction   90

7 The Reckoning   128

Notes   135

Bibliographical Essay   143

Index   153

ix

NATIONALISM IN BRAZIL

1. The Brazilian Concept of Nationalism

Authorities on nationalism agree on two points: first, that nationalism as a force is potent, and second, that nationalism as a concept is difficult to define. On the one hand, nationalism has been the impetus for war, conquest, and destruction. On the other, it has been the inspiration for art, poetry, and economic development. A varied force, extremely complex in its motivations and manifestations, it can accomplish much good when used for positive ends; so too, when perverted, it can bring great misery upon its adherents.

Simply defined, nationalism is a deep love for one's own country coupled with a disregard if not dislike for other countries. An extraneous force or threat, an outside antagonism, can create, heighten, or sustain dedication to one's country of birth or adoption. This elementary nationalism springs from the basic "us" versus "them" conflict. A somewhat more sophisticated definition of nationalism is that of a group consciousness that attributes great value to the nation-state, to which unswerving devotion is tendered. The individual closely identifies with the state and feels that his well-being depends to a large extent, if not completely, on its well-being. In the twentieth century, nationalism has generally been regarded as an agreement among the inhabitants of a given area—who, for one reason or another, identify with one another—to maintain their unity, independence, and sovereignty and to pursue certain broad and mutually acceptable goals.

It is possible to identify certain factors that contribute to the development of nationalistic feelings. The nation usually occupies an integral territory and has a common language. Frequently, a majority of the inhabitants share the same religion, hold certain basic political ideals in common, and display similar traits of character. The exceptions are numerous, and not all nations—even those that have experienced the greatest surges of nationalism—possess all these factors. Nationalism can and does manifest itself even when a common language, religion, and territorial integrity are lacking. National character is, at best, difficult to define. Nevertheless, these factors seem to be the major ingredients that make nationalism possible.

The origins of nationalism can be traced back to the Hebrews and Greeks. The Hebrews introduced the concepts of the chosen people and the national mission in history. The Greeks developed similar ideas, as well as an intense loyalty to their political unit, the city-state. Nationalism—or concepts associated with it, such as unity and loyalty—was present to some extent in the Roman Empire and medieval Europe. It became more easily identifiable as the modern state began to take shape in the sixteenth century. The state gradually absorbed the loyalties formerly given to city, region, church, or overlord, and over the centuries it became the most powerful political institution. Modern nationalism took form during the French Revolution, when for the first time the loyalty of all classes was pledged to the national state. Thereafter, nationalism increasingly gained broad popular support.

The background for Brazilian nationalism lies, of course, in Europe. The motherland, Portugal, was the first of the modern European states to appear. It accomplished its territorial integration and demarcation by the mid-thirteenth century, and the monarchs moved to consolidate control of the nation. King Denis, during his long reign (1279–1325), curtailed the landholdings of the church and substituted Portuguese for Latin as the language of the court and the bureaucracy. The Aviz kings of the fifteenth century humbled the nobles and exerted greater authority over the church as they centralized and increased their power. The Portuguese maritime feats of the fifteenth and sixteenth centuries augmented native pride and inspired Luís de Camões' immortal epic of national prowess, *The Lusiads,* in 1572. The people identified ever more closely with the nation rather than with the dynasty, a tendency discernible in their flexibility in accepting new royal houses—Burgundy, Aviz, and Braganza—and in the increasing glorification of national rather than royal achievements.

The nationalist spirit in Brazil boasts a long history of development. Its course was facilitated by the fact that Brazil possesses to an unusual degree all the factors that favor the formation and growth of nationalism. The first is unity of territory. Brazil stretches unbroken from the Amazon in the north to the Rio de la Plata in the south, and from the Atlantic coast to the foothills of the Andes. The challenge of expansion and the settlement of the interior, which was a common goal for men of all regions and classes, encouraged national sentiments. The vast majority of the people speak Portuguese and are Roman Catholic. Their language differentiates them from their Spanish-speaking neighbors, and their religion was, during the sixteenth and seventeenth centuries, a rallying cry to expel European interlopers, who were generally Protestant. Most Brazilians share to a greater or lesser degree certain ideological preferences. The Brazilians lived under a monarchy throughout most of the nineteenth century, and were thus isolated from their republican neighbors during the formative period of Latin American nationalism. Yet, as the century progressed, internal conditions changed, and the majority accepted the substitution of a republic for the monarchy, a change that was accomplished without bloodshed in 1889. Little ideological conflict resulted, and the Brazilians transferred their loyalties to the new republic. Brazilians have generally worked for peaceful reform of their political structures; recourse to violence has been the exception. They have shown themselves to be unusually tolerant in their attitudes, whether in questions of politics, race, or religion.

The Brazilian national character is more difficult to define. Gilberto Freyre has emphasized, in his classic study *The Masters and the Slaves,* that the combination of three races, European, African, and Indian, resulted in the formation of a unique civilization. Nowhere in the hemisphere—nowhere in the world, for that matter—have the three races mixed together so freely and so extensively. Each has made contributions to the national language, diet, institutions, traditions, mores, and folklore. The result is a society distinct from any other in the world.

An American psychologist, John F. Santos, has described "the Brazilian way of life" as one that includes close family relationships, respect for individual liberties, and a wide tolerance of people and ideas.[1] On a popular plane, the fanatical devotion to *futebol* and *carnaval* (to a degree extraordinary even in Latin America), the gay, friendly smile, the love of music, dance, and conviviality, all suggest broad traits of character. Sérgio Buarque de Holanda, whose *Raízes do Brasil* (Roots of Brazil) ranks as one of the best interpretive studies of his country, believes that a major Brazilian contribution to world civilization is that of the "cordial man." He notes that foreigners visiting Brazil are always impressed by the affability, hospitality, and generosity of Brazilians, who he believes rank among the best behaved and gentlest people in the world.[2] The Brazilian has negative traits as well, of course. He loves to procrastinate, and talk is more important to him than action. He begins his projects enthusiastically, only to lose interest quickly. He tends to seek the *jeito*—the easy way out. He feels that rules are made to be broken rather than observed.

The novelist Aluízio de Azevedo drolly described the making of a Brazilian in his *O Cortiço,* first published in 1890 (translated into English as *A Brazilian Tenement*). The novel's Portuguese immigrant hero, Jeronymo, began his transformation when he started to enjoy a morning cup of strong black coffee. *Cachaça* (a native white rum) next conquered his palate. He became more contemplative and romantic, less conservative and prudent. Austerity surrendered to pleasure, severity to joviality, ambition to indolence. Codfish, potatoes, and boiled onions vanished from his menu to be replaced by stewed dried beef, black beans, and mandioca. Cleanliness and attention to personal appearance assumed new importance. Music seduced Jeronymo, who began to strum a guitar and to sing the captivating tunes of Bahia. He acquired a leisurely sense of time. Thus, according to Azevedo, he became "Brazilianized"—he had successfully adopted the Brazilian way of life.

These character traits, then, together with the factors of unbroken territory, a common language, a unifying religion, and shared ideological preferences, have formed the basis for Brazilian nationalism.

The first manifestations of "Brazilianism"—that is, a feeling of differentiation from others and unity among themselves —are difficult to ascertain precisely. Historians vary in their judgments on the origins of Brazilian nationalism. Some would trace the origins back to the time of discovery. "From the beginning, Brazil was not the same as Portugal," José Honório Rodrigues asserted in his recent essay on national values and aspirations.[3] Another contemporary nationalist, Barbosa Lima Sobrinho, in his investigation of the roots of Brazilian nationalism, also affirmed that when the first immigrants to Brazil understood that their interests no longer coincided with those of Portugal, their loyalty to the motherland ended and Brazilian nationalism began.[4]

Clearly the New World was markedly different from Europe. Brazil offered the European a strange climate and

geography, as well as a puzzling new man, the Indian. Those
differences influenced the newly arrived European, who generally accepted the prevailing "mentality and morality" of
the New World[5]—in other words, he adapted to the new conditions. Consequently, the new arrival ceased to be a European, and became instead a "moral mestizo"—combining and
compromising his European training and customs with the
demands of the new land. His sons became both moral and
physical mestizos. If the European could not persevere spiritually in Brazil, neither could he continue physically. In his
place appeared a new man, the combination first of the European and the Indian, and, later, of the European, the Indian, and the African. Thus, the Brazilian as an individual
appeared centuries before Brazil emerged as an independent
nation.

The differences between the colony and the metropolis
increased over the decades and contributed to a growing
feeling of pride on the part of the Brazilians in their common
land, traditions, and experience. Many of the new arrivals at
once began to praise and defend the tropical land of their
adoption.[6] They regarded Brazil as affectionately as if their
ancestral roots were there. They set the tone for succeeding
generations, and laid the foundation for the complex emotions of modern Brazilian nationalism.

The present study traces the history of the development
of Brazilian nationalism from colonial times to the present.
Its purposes are to serve as a general guide for the historical
study of Brazilian nationalism and to provide a broad basis
for understanding the potent force of nationalism in Brazil
today.

The development of Brazilian nationalism can be divided
into three periods: colonial nativism, nineteenth-century defensive nationalism, and twentieth-century offensive nationalism. The last period can be further subdivided into two

rather well-defined categories: political and cultural nationalism, which dominated the first three decades of the twentieth century, and economic nationalism, which came to the fore after the rise to power of Getúlio Vargas, in 1930. The intellectual elite have provided the major continuity for the three periods. In their role as literati, they have formulated nationalist doctrine and directed, later in alliance with the politicians, the course of nationalism. It is only during the twentieth century that the Brazilian masses have adopted those doctrines to any degree.

Nativism was an expression of the colonists' love of and pride in their land; however, their exaltation of Brazil did not necessarily imply antagonism toward Portugal. Nativism developed slowly in the sixteenth and seventeenth centuries but accelerated significantly in the eighteenth. It eventually evolved into nationalism.

Brazilians have been reluctant to define nationalism precisely, preferring to discuss the concept in more general terms. Their varying definitions show the complexity, perhaps the perversity, of coming to grips with the concept. Barbosa Lima Sobrinho regards it as the affirmation of the unity of interests of a group, accentuated by conflicts and outside antagonisms.[7] Elysio de Carvalho says simply that "nationalism is the love of the fatherland . . . an affirmation that Brazil for each of its sons is the highest motive for living."[8] Hermes Lima, a politician who held high office under the Goulart administration, has given an equally straightforward definition: "Nationalism is devotion to national interests, to the defense of those interests—national unity, independence, etc."[9] A more specific definition is that of the literary historian Júlio Barbuda: "A sentiment felt by a people who share the same political creed, who have for the patterns of thought the same language, for the fatherland the same area, for traditions the same experiences, for the

molds of civic morality the social manifestations of the same
race, nationalism is the emotional synthesis of the fatherland."[10]

In the nineteenth century, Brazilians became increasingly
aware that their country differed from others. To the degree
that they understood that difference, they manifested intense
devotion and loyalty to their nation. Their isolation from and
contrast with both their Spanish-speaking neighbors and
Europe intensified national feeling. British imperialism, the
Portuguese presence, and threats from Spanish America, particularly in the Rio de la Plata area, were external antagonisms that periodically intensified nationalism as a defensive
force. Throughout the nineteenth century, nationalism remained a relatively simple devotion to the fatherland and a
distrust of foreigners.

Toward the end of the century, prosperity and progress
brought changes in Brazil and an increase in the self-confidence of the Brazilians. More sure of themselves, they became bolder in their desires, plans, and efforts to improve
their nation. The intellectuals became critical of their home-
land. They pointed out faults and recommended changes.
Their intention was to create a better and stronger Brazil.
Under the direction of the intellectuals, the nationalists paid
less attention to foreign threats (which in reality had dimin-
ished, if not altogether disappeared) and more to making
internal improvements. They sought to destroy feudal institutions and colonial patterns, to liberate Brazil from foreign
control, and to develop a modern, industrialized, indigenous
society. Nationalism became an offensive force.

During the first three decades of the twentieth century, the
nationalists concentrated primarily on political and cultural
questions. Encouraged by the intellectuals, they sought to
define and to cultivate the national culture, keeping it as free
as possible from foreign impurities. In this way they hoped
to awaken the national self-consciousness. They also organ-

ized ephemeral political parties, which appeared and disappeared with bewildering rapidity in the 1920's. With the Vargas era, the emphasis of the nationalists shifted to economic problems. Two of the leading Brazilian authorities on contemporary nationalism, Cândido Mendes de Almeida and Hélio Jaguaribe, have defined nationalism as an instrument for change and the key to development.[11] Thanks partly to their efforts, nationalism has come to furnish the philosophical basis for development, and thus it offers hope for a brighter future. Nelson Werneck Sodré alluded to these concepts when he wrote:

> Why Nationalism? Because now foreign economic forces are the greatest obstacle to our development and their internal allies decline in power, they no longer hold the nation in tutelage. For any country with a colonial past, with an economic structure subordinated to foreign interests, to create itself nationally is to accomplish a task in many ways similar to that which the European nations accomplished at the dawn of the Modern Age with the defeat of feudalism and the advance of capitalism. What for them were feudal relations, restrictions on development, are for us all that still remains of the colonial past. Nationalism presents itself as liberation.[12]

Sodré's final words provide the key to understanding the nationalist mentality of mid-twentieth-century Brazil. Nationalism promises to liberate Brazil from the past and to propel it into the future. This confidence in nationalism as an agent of change will become more apparent through a study of its development, which is traced in the following chapters.

2. The Formation of Brazil and the Cult of Nativism

In 1500, Pedro Alvares Cabral discovered Brazil, while off course on his route to India. To inform King Manoel I of Portugal of the unexpected discovery, Cabral's scribe, Pero Vaz de Caminha, composed a glowing report of the new land, which he described as "beautiful," "healthful," and "temperate." He assured his sovereign that "the country is so well-favored that if it were rightly cultivated it would yield everything." To Caminha the land was a veritable Garden of Eden. He was equally impressed by the inhabitants. "Truly these people are good and have a fine simplicity," he marveled. Above all, they were "innocent."[1] The letter of Caminha set the tone for future descriptions of the new land, and the Portuguese who arrived in Brazil thereafter were generally enthusiastic about what they saw.

The early chronicles, such as the *Diário da Navegação* (Navigation Diary) of Pero Lopes de Sousa and the *Tratado da Terra do Brasil* (Treatise on the Land of Brazil) of Pero de Magalhães de Gândavo, as well as private letters and official reports, praised the richness and potential of the American colony; all expressed optimism about its future. No group was more enthusiastic than the Jesuits, sent out in 1549 to carry Iberian church-centered civilization to Portuguese America. One early Jesuit correspondent believed that the land only needed settlers in order to flourish,[2] an observation that would be repeated over the centuries. Typical of nativistic sentiment in sixteenth-century Brazil is the following extract from a letter written by a Jesuit:

> And for the love of Christ, I ask you to lose the bad opinion which you have of Brazil, because I tell you truly that if there is paradise here on earth, I would say that it is in Brazil. And if I feel this way, I do not know anyone here who does not. . . . There is no healthier place in the world; fresh air, pleasant countryside, another like it cannot be found; the foods I think are better than those in Portugal, or at least that is my opinion, and truly I never even have a desire for any of the food there. If there are chickens in Portugal, here there are more and they are cheaper; if there is livestock in Portugal, here there are so many animals which they hunt in the forest and they have such delicious meat that I laugh to think of those in Portugal. If there is wine in Portugal, here there is delicious water everywhere which I find superior to the wines there. . . . Anyone who elects to live in a terrestrial paradise must come to live in Brazil, at least that is my opinion. And whoever does not believe me, let him come here and try it for himself.[3]

Throughout most of the sixteenth century, the colonists were too busy repelling the French, Dutch, and English trespassers, carving out their farms, plantations, and ranches, and protecting them from Indian attacks, to devote much time to philosophizing on their country and their relations to it. By the second century of colonization, however, the coast had been conquered, the Indians (those who had not been killed) driven inland or reduced to servitude, and sugar cultivated as a lucrative export crop. Only then could the Brazilians, as the colonists were known by that time, begin to reflect on themselves and their surroundings.

In his *Diálogos das Grandezas do Brasil* (Dialogues on the Greatness of Brazil), written in 1618, Ambrósio Fernandes Brandão made the first attempt to define and interpret Brazil. Brandão catalogued the vast natural resources of the colony and concluded that Brazil contained unbounded wealth. To the European charge that Brazil was a "vile land," he retorted: "Is that the fault of the country itself or of its inhabitants?" The question was rhetorical, of course. It could not be otherwise in a land "so fertile that every variety of crop in the world could be raised here; the climate is good, the heavens smiling, the temperature mild, the air wholesome; and it has a thousand other pleasing attributes as well." Any deficiencies lay therefore in the inhabitants, "who do not make use of the possibilities that are offered them."[4] As he struggled to define Brazil, Brandão's love for the colony was clearly evident. That search for self-identification which he initiated at the beginning of the seventeenth century became more pronounced through the years and, as we shall see, is a well-established characteristic of twentieth-century nationalism.

The Franciscan friar Vicente do Salvador, a native Brazilian, made the second important intellectual contribution to the nativism of the century by writing, in 1627, the first history of Brazil. His very Portuguese—a vocabulary infused with Indian words—revealed Brazilian linguistic influences. Not one to hide his pride in his native land, he boasted of its favorable location, its gigantic size, the wealth of its sugar industry, the potential population it could support. Frei Vicente assured his readers that Brazil could exist satisfactorily in isolation from the rest of the world, such were the variety and extent of its products and resources. In the optimistic tradition of the early chroniclers, he prophesied: "This will be a great kingdom."[5] Like Brandão, Frei Vicente set the course for future national self-examination.

While the intellectuals were beginning to discover and to analyze their own land, the Dutch, coveting the wealth of the sugar-rich tropics of South America, attacked the northeastern coast. They seized the capital of the colony, Bahia de Todos os Santos, in 1624. After being expelled the following year, they turned their attention to the economic capital, the prosperous captaincy of Pernambuco, which they took in

1630. Eventually they overran the fertile sugar lands between the mouths of the São Francisco and Amazon rivers. The Brazilians naturally resented the presence of the northern European heretics in their territory. The Portuguese, however, were too much absorbed in their own struggle for independence to pay much heed to events in the New World. When the last of the Aviz kings died, in 1580, leaving no heir, Philip II of Spain successfully pressed his claim to the Portuguese crown. The two Iberian kingdoms remained united until Portugal declared and won its independence in 1640. For several decades, the frontier with Spain absorbed Portuguese attention. To a large extent, then, the Brazilians were left alone to face the Dutch invaders. On their own, they began an intensive guerrilla warfare against the Dutch; in the war of liberation that followed, they fought practically unaided by the motherland.

The Dutch threat succeeded in solidifying the Brazilians into a union they had previously been unable to attain. The struggle against a common enemy lasted nearly a generation and brought together men from São Paulo, Rio de Janeiro, Bahia, Pernambuco, and Maranhão—in short, from all the inhabited areas of the far-flung colony. White man, Negro, Indian, and the resulting mixture of the white with those two races, the mulatto and the *caboclo,* marched side by side. The heroes of the struggle, men like Henrique Dias, Felipe Camarão, João Fernandes Vieira, and André Vidal, represented all the ethnic elements contributing to the creation of Brazil. Although heterogeneous in race and regional origin, they had in common their hatred of the Protestant Dutch and their devotion to Catholic Brazil. Furthermore, place of birth united them: they were sons of the New World. Their determination brought about the brilliant victories over the Dutch at Guararapes in 1648 and 1649; in 1654, they at last expelled the powerful invaders.

The victory increased the pride of the Brazilians and gave

them a confidence they had previously lacked. No longer did the *mazombos*, the native-born Brazilians, consider themselves the inferiors of the *reinóis*, those born in Portugal. The victory over the great maritime power of Northern Europe immensely encouraged the growth of Brazilian nationalism. Brazilian historians generally point to the defeat of the Dutch as a turning point in the growth of national feeling.[6] Elysio de Carvalho summed up this view when he remarked: "From the epic of the Reconquest onward, the evolution of national sentiment can be defined as a firm, continuous, and growing affirmation of our consciousness of being a people."[7] João Capistrano de Abreu, the foremost historian of the colonial period, went even farther. He concluded that in the victory over the Dutch "the national spirit emerged victorious. . . . External pressure brought about a unity, superficial and imperfect, but at least the start of a unity of the diverse ethnic elements."[8]

Anti-Lusitanian feeling also dates from this period. The *mazombos* disliked those *reinóis* who arrived in the New World to exploit it and then return with their riches to Portugal. The failure of the Portuguese to contribute wholeheartedly to the defeat of the Dutch heightened the antagonism of the colonists. The seventeenth-century Bahian poet Gregório de Matos gave voice to this resentment. He was not only one of the most vocal of the nativists but one of the first to define the growing dislike the Brazilians felt toward the Portuguese. In his poem "Portuguese of the Realm," he showed his scorn for the newly arrived immigrants from the metropolis:

> Is there a miracle more strange—
> Hear me well, you who have ears—
> Than a man from Lisbon or Minho Province,
> A Kingdom worthy, who in our midst appears?
> Some lad who flees his father's wrath,

A criminal who here must roam;
Or else he comes that he may eat,
For there is nothing to eat at home.
Barefoot, naked save for his rags—
Ah, there upon the wharf he springs;
And a few lice and filthy bags
Are all the capital he brings.[9]

His biting and witty criticism would be repeated over the centuries and is the ancestor of the innumerable jokes Brazilians still tell that have as their butt the Portuguese immigrant.

Native resentment of the outsider turned into open conflict in the Wars of the Emboabas and of the Mascates early in the eighteenth century. The first war broke out in 1708–09 in Minas Gerais. It was essentially a struggle between the residents of the Brazilian interior and the fortune hunters newly arrived from the coast and the motherland (the "foreigners" were pejoratively termed *emboabas* by the locals). The second war, which erupted in 1710–11, was provoked by the bitter rivalry between the native landed aristocracy centered in Olinda and the aggressive Portuguese merchants in neighboring Recife (who were called *mascates*, or "peddlers," by the natives). If once the Portuguese-born had disdained the *caboclo* and the *mazombo*, the tables had turned. The Brazilian-born now spurned the metropolitan. A far-reaching psychological change was occurring in the Brazilians.

One of the most dynamic aspects of Brazilian development in the seventeenth and eighteenth centuries was territorial expansion. By the Treaty of Tordesillas (1494), which divided the world between Spain and Portugal, only the eastern bulge of South America became Portuguese territory. The Luso-Brazilians soon began to penetrate inland beyond the narrow treaty confines. Spain's failure to protest the expansion of its neighbor was construed as tacit acquiescence in that expansion.

The men most directly responsible for the extension of Brazil's frontiers were the *bandeirantes,* a hearty group of adventurous *caboclos* who restlessly explored the interior in search of Indian slaves and gold. Around the year 1695, gold was discovered in the area that became known as Minas Gerais (General Mines). The gold rush that followed turned the eyes of Portugal and the colony from the coast to the interior. It also encouraged further exploitation of the interior. New gold lodes were uncovered in Goiás and Mato Grosso. Diamonds and other precious stones were also discovered. Proud of their expansion from the Atlantic Ocean to the foothills of the Andes, the Luso-Brazilians sought legal recognition of their territorial acquisition. It was a Brazilian, Alexandre de Gusmão, who helped to formulate Portuguese frontier diplomacy in South America. The happy result of his counsel was the Treaty of Madrid of 1750, which by and large defined the boundaries between Portuguese and Spanish America on the basis of *uti possidetis* (ownership through occupation), thereby recognizing the expansion of the *bandeirantes*. The configuration of Brazil has remained essentially the same to the present day.

At the same time that Brazil was taking physical form, typical Brazilian types were appearing. The hardy, half-caste *bandeirante,* suspicious of government control, eager for freedom, was, of course, an indigenous figure. So were the horse-loving *vaqueiros,* the cowboys of the Northeast, and the *gaúchos,* their counterparts of the extreme South. Still another type that had appeared by the eighteenth century was the *tropeiro.* This wandering merchant, his mules loaded with merchandise, crisscrossed the colony carrying news, gossip, and customs, as well as the European goods from the ports. These and other types were peculiar to Brazil and had no counterparts in Portugal.

A native aristocracy also emerged. At its head stood the powerful and patriarchal *senhor de engenho,* the owner of immense cane fields and bustling sugar mills. Born and raised in the New World, the colonial aristocrats owned much of the property and dominated the local government. Their interests and ambitions prompted them to identify much more closely with Brazil than with the distant metropolis. They looked upon their own accomplishments as well as those of their land with a growing pride.

As the *bandeirantes* from Belém, São Luís, Recife, Bahia, Rio de Janeiro, and São Paulo,.followed by missionaries, cattlemen, and *tropeiros,* penetrated the interior, they broke down the regionalism of the isolated coastal populations. Moving northward from São Paulo, *bandeirantes* established cattle ranches in Piauí and Maranhão. Cattlemen from Pernambuco made the long ride to sell their herds to the miners of Minas Gerais. Missionaries from the coastal convents descended on the West and North, attempting to save the Indians from enslavement. In the interior all types and conditions of men mixed, and the shared hardships created a common experience that submerged their regional origins and loyalties. Throughout the country's history, the vast interior has played a vital role in substituting the Brazilian for the Paulista, the Bahiano, the Pernambucano, and the Maranhense.

To the physical creation of boundaries and population was added the spiritual formation of an emerging nation. The native intellectual elite, concentrated in the small but growing urban centers, continued to study themselves, their environment, and their past. As frequently happens in new countries, an inferiority complex prompted the literati to exaggerated boasting. Their lavish praise of local traditions and the natural beauty of their land stimulated that cultural pride which is an early manifestation of nationalism. Although few in number, they wielded a disproportionately powerful influence.

The Bahian Jesuit André João Antonil initiated the eighteenth-century movement to glorify Brazil with his highly descriptive *Cultura e Opulência do Brasil* (The Culture and Opulence of Brazil). Published in 1711 in Lisbon (there was as yet no printing press in colonial Brazil), Antonil's treatise was promptly suppressed by the royal authorities, who feared that it revealed too much to prying foreign eyes—or, perhaps, that it might further stimulate the growth of local pride. The crown did not wish either to tempt anew any European power to trespass on its American domains or to encourage any Brazilian nationalist aspirations. Antonil spoke in no uncertain terms of the colony's wealth. *Cultura e Opulência* was much less defensive and far more boastful than was the seventeenth-century *Diálogos das Grandezas do Brasil,* and evidenced the swelling nativism of the eighteenth-century literati. Nuno Marques Pereira continued in a similar vein in his *Compêndio Narrativo do Peregrino da América* (The Narrative of an American Pilgrim), of 1728. The American pilgrim of the title made an overland journey from São Paulo to Bahia. As he wandered, he commented on the geography, history, and customs of Brazil, describing the land in florid language: "The densely tufted groves, the fragrant flowers, the spacious meadows all covered with fine silver in the form of those pearls with which the opulent dawn enriches it at no stint to herself."

The classic example of the nativist literature of glorification remains the *História da América Portuguêsa, 1500–1724* (History of Portuguese America), by Sebastião da Rocha Pita. When the first Brazilian academy, the Academia dos Esquecidos (the Academy of the Forgotten), was founded in Bahia in 1724, in imitation of the European academies of the day, Rocha Pita was a charter member. He took quite seriously the goal of the Academy: to write a history of Brazil. The group disbanded in 1725, but Rocha Pita carried out its great project. His history, the first since that of Frei Vicente do Salvador a century earlier, was published in Lisbon in 1730. The title might suggest some loyalty to the motherland, but the contents were undeniably nativistic. The author displayed an unmistakable pride in the growth of the colony,[10] and his style was typical of that of the nativists:

> Of the New World . . . Brazil comprises the major part. It is a vast region with favored terrain. On its soil grow all fruits; in its subsoil exist all treasures. Its mountains and coasts abound with pleasant air. Its fields give the most useful food; its mines, the finest gold; its tree trunks, the smoothest balsam; its seas, the most select amber. It is an admirable country, rich in every respect, where prodigiously profuse nature sacrifices herself in fertile produce for the opulence of the monarchy and the benefit of the world by shooting forth its sugar cane to be squeezed into nectar and by giving as its fruits ripe ambrosia, the liquor and meat the cultured populace offered to its false gods.
>
> In no other region is the sky more serene or the dawn which greets the day more beautiful; the sun in no other hemisphere has such golden rays nor the nocturnal reflections more brilliance; the stars here are more benign and always joyous; the horizons where the sun rises and sets are always bright; the waters, whether in the fountains of the countryside or in the aqueducts of the city are the purest anywhere; in short, Brazil, where the mighty rivers surge and flow, is an earthly paradise.[11]

An even more nativistic historian than Rocha Pita was Pedro Taques de Almeida Paes Leme, who wrote of the common people of Brazil, not of the Portuguese viceroys and bishops. In various works, such as *Nobiliarquia Paulistana* (Paulista Geneology), he praised the Paulistas and their prowess in conquering the land.

Other historians who displayed nativistic tendencies were José Mirales, Frei Antônio de Santa Maria Jaboatão, Frei

Gaspar da Madre de Deus, Antônio José Vitorino Borges da Fonseca, and Frei Domingos do Loreto Couto. In his *História Militar do Brasil* (Military History of Brazil), Mirales recounted (in none-too-modest fashion) the feats of the Luso-Brazilians from 1549 to 1762. Jaboatão's *Novo Orbe Seráphico ou Chrônica dos Frades Menores da Província do Brasil* (New Heavenly Sphere, or Chronicle of the Minor Orders of the Province of Brazil) was primarily a religious history, but it ranged over the entire course of Brazil's development. In his *Memórias para a História da Capitania de São Vicente* (Notes for a History of the Captaincy of São Vicente), Frei Gaspar emphasized the achievements of the southerners in the development of Brazil. Borges da Fonseca wrote four volumes containing biographies of Pernambucans—*Nobiliarquia Pernambucana* (Pernambucan Geneology)—who emerge as heroes wresting wealth from the wilderness. Loreto Couto praised the Indian, foreshadowing the romantic concept of the noble savage that would prevail in Brazil during the following century. His *Desagravos do Brasil e Glórias de Pernambuco* (Redresses of Brazil and Glories of Pernambuco) frankly sought to call attention to the achievements of the colony.

The second half of the eighteenth century also witnessed the appearance of the works of two epic poets, José Basílio da Gama and José de Santa Rita Durão. Basílio da Gama's *O Uraguai,* a poem in blank verse, was written in the late 1760's. The poem tells of the heroic resistance of the Indians of seven missionary villages of southern Brazil to both Spanish and Portuguese incursions. It also presents a charming picture of the Brazilian landscape. In his exaltation of the noble qualities of the Indian, Basílio da Gama, like Loreto Couto, was a precursor of the nineteenth-century, romantic Indianist movement in Brazilian literature. Santa Rita Durão's epic poem *Caramurú,* published in 1781, traces the history of the colony from discovery to the expulsion of the last foreign invader. (The title of the poem refers to the name the Indians gave to a shipwrecked Portuguese sailor who lived among them, adopted their customs, and later became their leader.) Written in ottava rima, the poem treats of the political and natural history of the colony.[12] The historian João Ribeiro and the literary critic Sílvio Romero have both called *Caramurú* "the most Brazilian poem we possess."[13]

Although more timid than the writers and poets, Brazilian artists were not totally insensitive to the local scene. The mulatto painter Jesuino do Monte Carmelo included a smiling mulatto cherub among a host of white angels he painted on the ceiling of the church of the Carmelite Brotherhood in Itú, São Paulo. The Jesuits at missions along the Uruguay River erected a statue of St. George, trampling beneath his feet not a dragon, but a *bandeirante* slave-hunter from São Paulo.

The most original Brazilian art, however, was the work of a mulatto cripple, Antônio Francisco Lisboa, known as "Aleijadinho" ("The Little Cripple"). His haunting sculptures executed in eighteenth-century Minas Gerais owe little to European inspiration. Often disproportionate and malshaped, they reflect his own sufferings and prejudices and convey a strong impression of human feeling.

In the last decades of the eighteenth century, Brazilian naturalists for the first time began to catalog scientifically the wealth of the subcontinent. The most outstanding of these was Alexandre Rodrigues Ferreira, who traveled throughout the vast Amazon region from 1783 to 1793 and left a voluminous record of his observations. His principal work, *Diário da Viagem Filosófico* (Diary of a Philosophical Trip), called attention to the untapped resources and potential of the Amazon. In 1790, the Franciscan friar José Mariano da Conceição Veloso completed his study *Flora Fluminense*. Based on eight years of research, the book catalogued and described 1,640 plants indigenous to the captaincy of Rio de Janeiro.

In the decades that followed, an entire literature appeared in which Brazilians discussed the abundance nature had bequeathed them.

By the end of the eighteenth century, the intellectual elite had created a spiritual foundation for Brazil, and the nativism they expounded accelerated the alienation of the Brazilians from the Portuguese. The work of the intellectuals provided the basis for the observation of Sílvio Romero that "the poets and historians are the active priests officiating over the soul of nationality."[14] Júlio Barbuda has also emphasized the connection between the creation of nationality and the cultivation of literature.[15] The literati had created, then, the necessary psychological setting for independence. In the case of Brazil, it was true, to use the expression of Hélio Jaguaribe, that "the nation in the historical sense preceded the nation in the political sense."[16]

Other Latin American historians concur in that opinion. The Mexican Daniel Cosío Villegas believed that Spanish and Portuguese colonial oppression created a "nationalist sentiment and ardor" foreshadowing Latin American independence.[17] The Peruvian Víctor Andrés Belaúnde spoke of a "colonial nationalism" found throughout the hemisphere by the beginning of the nineteenth century.[18] Another Peruvian, Jorge Basadre, wrote that "in this sense, the *conciencia de sí,*' the national self-consciousness felt by Americans . . . first appeared in the late seventeenth century and reached maturity in the early decades of the nineteenth century."[19] These historians have pointed out a significant key to the understanding of the formation of at least some of the Latin American states, and certainly of Brazil: they existed spiritually—and emotionally—for some time before they existed politically.

As the eighteenth century drew to a close, the native elite ceased to be content with simply praising the land of their birth. They felt around them the pressures for revolution.

The English colonies to the north had freed themselves from the motherland and were demonstrating new vigor and growth. The rallying cries of the French Revolution were reverberating through the continent. Then Spanish America burst into flames, destroying the ties between the New World and Spain. In Brazil, there had been extensive economic development, and the maturing of the colony prompted the Brazilian intellectuals to take action. They led political protests and codified economic complaints, but were probably more effective in the latter.

One of the first to protest the economic restrictions placed on Brazil was the Brazilian-born Bishop José Joaquim da Cunha de Azeredo Coutinho. Three of Coutinho's works are notable for voicing some of the most frequent complaints of the colonials. The first, *Memória sôbre o Preço do Açúcar* (Memorial on the Price of Sugar), published in 1791, attacked the proposed tax on sugar, Brazil's principal export and the source of most of the colony's wealth. The second, *Ensaio Econômico sôbre o Comércio de Portugal e suas Colônias* (1794), published in English in 1807 under the title *An Essay on the Commerce and Products of the Portuguese Colonies in South America, Especially the Brazils,* examined the burdens placed on Brazil's trade. The abolition of the salt monopoly alone, the bishop-economist predicted, would give rise to new economic activity far more valuable to Brazil than all the mines of Potosí. Finally, *Discurso sôbre o Estado Atual das Minas do Brasil* (A Discussion of the Present State of the Mines of Brazil) (1804) criticized the outmoded methods of mining employed in Brazil and called for the introduction of more scientific methods into that industry. A chorus of other economic dilettantes soon joined Azeredo Coutinho. One of the most enlightened was the Bahian João Rodrigues de Brito. Writing in the first decade of the nineteenth century on the slow progress in Brazilian agriculture, Brito concluded:

In order for the farmers to achieve the full liberty which the well-being of agriculture demands, it is necessary for them to have: (1) the liberty to grow whatever crops they deem best, (2) the liberty to construct whatever works and factories they judge necessary for the good of their crops, (3) the liberty to sell in any place, by any means, and through whatever agent they wish to without heavy taxes or any bureaucracy, (4) the liberty to sell to those buyers who offer the highest prices, and (5) the liberty to sell their products at any time when it best suits them. Unfortunately, the farmers of the captaincy [Bahia] enjoy none of these liberties at the present time.[20]

Brito also commented on the political aspects of development: "All these beneficial instructions will amount to little and fail to spread human knowledge without the liberty to think freely and to publish those thoughts by all the means known, principally the press."[21] This was a daring statement in a colony where the formation and expression of opinion had the benefit of neither a single printing press nor a university. The Brazilians were becoming more openly critical of their government, while at the same time even more optimistic about the potential of their land.

The intellectuals did not limit themselves to observation and writing, however. They were ripe for political action as well. Intellectuals prepared and led the *Inconfidência*, a somewhat romantic independence plot quashed in Minas Gerais in 1789, and an unsuccessful revolution in Pernambuco in 1817. One young and idealistic rebel connected with the *Inconfidência*, José Joaquim Maia, wrote to Thomas Jefferson in 1786: "The men of letters are those who most desire a revolution."[22] There was one notable exception to this statement—the "Revolt of the Tailors," a Bahian *inconfidência* (as all the revolutionary plots were known) of 1798. The majority of the persons implicated in the bizarre plot to set up a local republic were simple artisans who had been moved by the ideas of the Enlightenment. The abortive revolt was the sole instance of a popular uprising for political independence in Brazil.

In 1807, Napoleon's invasion of Portugal forced the Portuguese royal family to flee to the New World. The monarch found Rio de Janeiro to his liking and remained there until 1821, when English and Portuguese pressure forced him to return to Europe. His long residence in Brazil temporarily cooled the ardor for independence. At the same time, however, the foundation of new schools, academies, and cultural institutions, and the elevation of Brazil to the status of a kingdom, in 1815, encouraged native pride. A British merchant, John Luccock, who resided in Rio de Janeiro during the eventful years 1808–18, left a record of the changing outlook and attitudes of the Brazilians of the time. Luccock discussed the beneficial effects of the 1808 decree that opened Brazilian ports to world trade, commenting on the "wonderful alteration it produced in the people's views and modes of thinking." He discussed the salutary effect of raising Brazil to the status of a kingdom:

> . . . the stimulus most prompt and efficacious in promoting the internal improvement of which we are speaking, particularly in forming a national character and feeling, of which Brazil was almost destitute, and for want of which the country had nearly fallen, like the colonies of Spain, into a number of disjointed states, arose out of the measure which gave to this important part of the Portuguese Domains privileges and honours similar to those enjoyed by the mother country. The period for assuming this new distinction, under the title of the United Kingdom of Portugal, Brazil, and Algarva, was judiciously fixed for the anniversary of the Queen's birth-day, in December, 1815. All were pleased with the circumstance, and though the projectors evidently saw little more in it than a change of title, the people felt that they entered upon a new era of their political existence, appeared to think themselves elevated to a higher rank in the scale of human beings, beheld an irrefragable proof that their destiny was fixed—that Brazil would, in future, be con-

sidered as one of the nations of the world, and be no longer sacrificed to the interests of any other state. The event infused into the public mind a sense of independence, a proper consciousness of its own importance, and a determination to support the new dignity.[23]

Luccock also pointed out the singular importance of the presence of the royal court in Brazil in unifying the colony and in arousing native pride.

This feeling of Nationality was still further promoted, soon afterwards, by an event of a different nature. Within a few months [in 1816] Brazil had to mourn the death of its first Queen, whose funeral obsequies being celebrated by every city, town, and considerable village in the Kingdom, called the people again together, and their attention fixed upon one common subject. On this occasion they displayed all the talent for show, all the taste for decoration, sculpture, oratory, and verse, which the country possessed. By such attractions the Brazilians were induced to leave, for a time, their recesses in woods and deserts, to assemble in the principal towns of their districts, become better acquainted with each other, and with their rulers; they acquired and riveted new degrees of civilization, new attachment to the Sovereign, who was already known, and had been beloved as Regent.[24]

The growth of a national consciousness, which Luccock so accurately noted, had its inevitable triumph in the proclamation of Brazil's independence in 1822. Members of the Brazilian elite, transformed from bucolic nativists into radical nationalists, helped to create and swore to defend a sovereign nation. Brazil sprang forth and grew as a unified nation thanks at least in part to virile nativism or precocious nationalism. A national sentiment among the native-born elite, and a vague feeling of devotion to their native land among scattered segments of the masses, help to explain why that gigantic country, unlike the other huge administrative areas of colonial Latin America, did not fragment after independence.[25]

3. *The Defensive Nationalism of the Nineteenth Century*

Independence came swiftly, almost painlessly, to Brazil. When King João VI returned to Lisbon in 1821, he left behind his impetuous young son, Pedro, to govern Brazil. Although surrounded by Portuguese advisers, the prince fell under the influence of some ardent Brazilian nationalists, the most prominent of whom was José Bonifácio de Andrada e Silva. Pedro listened sympathetically to their complaints and aspirations. In January, 1822, he appointed José Bonifácio as his Minister of the Interior. At the same time, the Portuguese Côrtes, resentful of the exalted position Brazil had come to occupy in the empire, moved to reduce the country to its former colonial status. The Brazilians refused to return to the past. Under the leadership of José Bonifácio, the elite exerted pressure on the impressionable Prince to defy the Côrtes. Their emotions swept Pedro along the course to independence. On January 9, 1822, he refused to obey the order of the Côrtes to return to Lisbon. In May, he announced that no act of the Côrtes would have force in Brazil without his approval. At the behest of the municipal government of Rio de Janeiro, the local Masonic Lodges, and the nationalists, he took the title "Perpetual Defender of Brazil." Then, in early September, while traveling to São Paulo, Pedro received notification from the Côrtes that it was reasserting its power over Brazil and reducing his authority. The Prince reacted immediately. Standing on the banks of the Ypiranga river, he raised his sword and cried: "Independence or death!" That cry, on September 7, 1822, marked the political severance of the 4 million Brazilians from the metropolis. It was the climax of three centuries of changing attitudes toward Portugal—from inferiority, to equality, to superiority.

Independence became effective principally because of a temporary alliance between the planter aristocracy and the new urban elite, two groups that had cultivated nativism. Both expressed pride in the achievements of Brazil and scorn for Portugal, and both stood to gain handsomely from independence. The planters desired greater freedom of trade in order to expand their overseas markets. They feared Portuguese restrictions on their local powers and distrusted the government in Lisbon. The emerging urban elite occupied an insecure position between the plantation owners and the slaves. This restless group felt that independence was the best way to improve its status. Many members of this class became ministers, deputies, and functionaries in the new government. The agreement of these two controlling elements of Brazilian society that independence was necessary and desirable meant that Pedro's unilateral declaration could —and did—become effective.

Yet, because of the rapidity with which independence was declared and established, the nation came into existence without any need to define itself. There was, in effect, no belligerent mother country to oppose. Hence, there was scant impetus to create a "Brazilianist" rationale to explain the existence of the new state. During the protracted war between the thirteen North American colonies and England, for example, the Americans developed an elaborate explanation for their action. Political theorists explained the struggle and the reasons for it, couching those explanations in patriotic phrases that aroused the "nationalist" spirit of the people; a general consensus on future political action was formed during the Revolutionary War. The long and bitter war waged in Spanish South America gave Simón Bolívar and his followers ample opportunity to prepare a number of programs of action, all of which provided at least some ideological base for the new nations.

In Brazil, no such revolutionary program emerged. The diffuse nativistic sentiments were no substitute for political and economic doctrines and programs. Epic poems and Gongoristic praise had been perfect for the *salons,* and they had undeniably served their purpose well. But after 1822, the new nation needed a firmer ideological base upon which to build; yet no nationalist doctrine appeared. Thus, for some time Brazilian nationalism failed to focus sharply. National consciousness was limited mainly to scattered intellectuals and politicians. Much of Brazil—particularly those vast areas outside the coastal cities—seemed only vaguely and imperfectly aware of its own existence.

The few moments of strength known to nineteenth-century Brazilian nationalism resulted either from foreign threats— real or imagined—to the young empire, or from foreign cultural domination. The direct challenges—military, political, and economic—which came primarily from Portugal, Great Britain, and Spanish America, were felt by Brazilians to threaten both their sovereignty and their unity. At those times, waves of anti-Portuguese, anti-British, and anti-Spanish American sentiment swept over Brazil, and nationalist feelings inevitably surged up. The intellectuals, who were the chief spokesmen for nationalist sentiments, also resented the influence Europe exerted over the psychological formation of their nation. This cultural hegemony provoked cries of protest and somewhat feeble and confused attempts to substitute an indigenous culture. Thus, throughout the nineteenth century, Brazilian nationalism tended to be a reaction to foreign events or attitudes. Yet although it was primarily introverted and defensive, it nevertheless helped Brazil to assert its political independence, to maintain national unity, and to press its territorial claims.

Antipathy toward Portugal, of course, predated independence. The Brazilians inherited their anti-Lusitanian attitudes from the former *reinóis-mazombos* rivalries, the historical continuation of the sentiments expressed by Gregório de Matos and apparent in the War of the Mascates. After João VI returned to Lisbon, the vindictiveness of the Côrtes set off vicious anti-Portuguese demonstrations in the major Brazilian cities. The new and irresponsible Brazilian press fanned the flames of hatred. The Constituent Assembly, convened in 1823 to write the empire's first constitution, was composed of the Brazilian-born, and it became a center of agitation against all things and persons Portuguese. Even the new Emperor, who had been born in Portugal, did not escape criticism. Although he had been brought to Brazil at the age of nine, his birth made him suspect among the nationalists. In the struggle between Portugal and Brazil, Pedro had sided with Brazil and had won the Brazilians' admiration. But in the ensuing rivalry between the native Brazilians and those of Portuguese birth living in Brazil, the young Emperor appeared to favor the latter, and that preference eventually cooled the ardor of his Brazilian-born supporters. Pedro's insistence on appointing men born in Portugal to high government office outraged the native Brazilians, and in particular the influential elite, who had hoped to fill those positions themselves. The fact that Pedro was the legitimate heir to the Portuguese throne heightened their suspicions. To the nationalists, he seemed to display a taste for wearing both crowns at once, thereby reuniting the two nations in his person. He never overcame those suspicions and they were the major cause of his abdication. In his abdication statement, on April 7, 1831, Pedro I showed that he was well aware of the anti-Portuguese attitudes threatening his retention of the throne:

> I prefer to descend the throne with honor than to go on reigning as a sovereign who has been dishonored and degraded. Those born in Brazil no longer want me for the reason that I am Portuguese. I have been expecting this for a long time, have seen it coming ever since I visited Minas Gerais. My son has the advantage over me of being Brazilian by birth. The Brazilians respect him. He will have no difficulty in governing, and the Constitution guarantees him his rights. I renounce the crown with the glory of ending as I began—constitutionally.[1]

Pedro sailed to Europe to become involved in Portuguese dynastic struggles. Most of the Portuguese-born high officials left office with their patron. In that way the government of Brazil came for the first time into the hands of the Brazilians. In a certain respect, the abdication signified the real end of Portuguese rule and the beginning of meaningful Brazilian independence. Yet despite the fact that men linked to the native aristocracy held the principal offices after 1831, xenophobia continued to rage. It became a convenient tool to create national unity.

In the decades following the abdication, anti-Portuguese prejudices assumed economic characteristics as Brazil struggled to liberate itself from the Portuguese dominance of commerce. The Rio de Janeiro newspaper *O Jacobino,* stating "we fight and we hate the Portuguese," called for the confiscation of Portuguese property.[2] The inhabitants of the principal ports were particularly sensitive to the strong economic position of the Portuguese residents, who they felt profited at the expense of the Brazilians. Nowhere was this truer than in Recife, where the antipathy between the Brazilian citizenry and the Portuguese merchants recalled the atmosphere that had led to the War of the Mascates more than a century earlier. A typical economic nationalist of the mid-nineteenth century was Inácio Bento de Loiola, who edited Recife's *A Voz do Brasil,* a virulent anti-Lusitanian newspaper. In an editorial of October 27, 1847, Loiola summed up Brazilian feeling as follows:

> In effect twenty-six years have passed since we declared our independence and during this time only the foreigner has profited, only he has taken advantage of our resources, while at the same time our people become each day more miserable, more insulted, more exposed to scorn and derision. Look at the capital of the empire and at the other maritime cities of the country; notice that alluvium of foreigners found in them; observe the influence that they exercise even in our politics; pay heed to their commercial monopolies, and finally consider the insolence with which these dangerous guests treat our people and you will know the misery of our situation.[3]

Words were followed by actions—such as the foundation in Recife in 1873 of the Society for the Nationalization of Commerce—but they were always too timid to be really effective.

If the Portuguese in effect enjoyed a monopoly over domestic commerce, the British soon obtained firm control of Brazil's international trade. As the protector of the Portuguese overseas empire from Napoleonic invasion, Great Britain had received from the Portuguese monarch (in a series of treaties dated 1810) a favored position in the Brazilian market. The duties on imports from England were lower than for any other nation, an arrangement guaranteeing British economic preeminence in Portuguese America. In addition, the English, who opposed slavery for both humanitarian and economic reasons, began to exert increasing pressure on Portugal to curtail the slave trade. A Brazilian intellectual and journalist living in London, Hipólito da Costa, initiated the first vigorous campaign against the treaties of 1810. His quixotic efforts failed. When Brazil declared its independence, the price for recognition by the Court of St. James's came high. Brazil had to agree, by treaties signed in 1827, to continue to give Britain a favored position in its markets, similar to that assured by the treaties of 1810, and to abolish the slave trade within three years. Pedro I paid the price asked for recognition, but not without the vociferous protests of the Brazilians. The 15 per cent tariff preference was grudgingly honored until it expired in 1844, when the Brazilians adamantly refused to renew it, despite heavy pressure from London. Instead, the government promulgated the first protective tariff, the Alves Branco Tariff of 1844. The Brazilians defied the treaty abolishing the slave trade. They were not ready to take that step, and external pressure only increased their determination to import slaves, which they continued to do until 1850.

Anti-British sentiment erupted twice in the last half of the century, when London challenged Brazilian sovereignty. The first incident was the so-called Christie affair of the mid-1860's, involving several complaints made to the imperial government by the British Minister to Brazil, William D. Christie. Christie accused the Brazilians of plundering a wrecked English ship on the coast of Rio Grande do Sul; he asked compensation for the stolen goods and punishment of the men responsible. He also demanded that the Brazilian government apologize for the arrest in Rio de Janeiro of three drunken British sailors and that it punish the police officials involved. When he failed to receive proper satisfaction, Christie ordered the British fleet to blockade Rio's Guanabara Bay; the British naval commander seized five Brazilian merchant ships. A rupture of diplomatic relations followed. The nation in general and the people of Rio de Janeiro in particular were indignant at their highhanded treatment by the English.

In 1895, the occupation of the Brazilian island Ilha de Trindade by the British Navy, for the purpose of establishing a submarine cable station, evoked a similar reaction and occasioned a flurry of diplomatic activity in Rio de Janeiro. The old fears of a foreign invasion of the vast, underpopulated territory of Brazil were awakened. Britain's initiative in re-establishing diplomatic relations with Brazil after Christie's hasty departure, and later the restitution of Trindade, meant that both affairs ended satisfactorily for Brazil, but not before they had stirred up renewed nationalist activity.

Anti-Spanish American feeling was intensified during the struggle to maintain Brazil's southern boundary on the left bank of the Rio de la Plata. Ever since the founding of Colô-nia do Sacramento, in 1680, the Brazilians had felt they must control at least one bank of the estuary, since the Rio de la Plata network was a primary means of communication and transportation for the entire south-central area of Brazil. That desire conflicted with the interests of Argentina, Uruguay, and Paraguay, which were loath to permit Brazilian control of a river of equal strategic importance to them. This clash of interests resulted in repeated interventions and even war-fare. The Cisplatine War, 1825–28, pitted Brazil against Ar-gentina over the future status of Uruguay. The War of the Triple Alliance, 1865–70, found Brazil, Argentina, and Uru-guay locked in a costly struggle with Paraguay. Brazil inter-vened repeatedly in Uruguay to guarantee its own Platine interests and in 1852 even intervened in Argentina to help overthrow the belligerent Juan Manuel Rosas.

Throughout the rest of the Second Empire, Brazil concen-trated its diplomatic energy on maintaining the precarious balance of power in the Plata area. Argentina, which had emerged as Brazil's chief rival in South America, was increas-ingly regarded with suspicion. In turn, the Argentines were wary of their neighbor's intentions. The nineteenth-century Argentine statesman Juan Bautista Alberdi denounced the Brazilians as "imperialists,"[4] and Brazil's neighbors, while un-able or unwilling to take concerted action against the Portu-guese-speaking giant in their midst, frequently repeated that charge. The protest against Brazilian expansionism was carried into the twentieth century, when Argentine nationalists warned Spanish Americans:

> The natural enemy of all the Hispanic-American nations is Brazil. It is our born enemy. . . . Speaking a different language, differently oriented in culture and politics, entirely different because of the mixture with the Negro race . . . Brazil forms a foreign element within our body.[5]

Brazilian nationalists responded in equally strong terms:

> Whether the Argentine sociologists like it or not, we have already proved the superiority of our organizational talents by systematizing juridic, economic, and intellectual forces, while the Hispanic inferiority becomes obvious in the fragmentation of states all more or less weak, all more or less turbulent. . . .
>
> The historic and political superiority of Brazil is manifest: united, colossal, irreducible. . . . It is destined to occupy in South America within a century the same preponderant place that the United States occupies in North America.[6]

Clearly, there was scant understanding and little friendship between Spanish and Portuguese America.

Those foreign threats and infringements, then, created national hatreds. Brazilians found themselves in the position of "us" versus "them," a situation conducive to exaggerated loyalty to the nation. Ultimately, outside pressures unified the population, strengthened the power of the central government, and contributed to the further sharpening of national consciousness.[7] In the face of foreign threats, the Brazilians —at least sporadically—had to define themselves, their position, and their national goals. Thus Barbosa Lima Sobrinho was led to conclude that "the substance of nationalism is an antagonism of interests or of ideas."[8]

On this point there is a curious paradox, however. The Brazilians were suspicious of the foreigner and not infrequently disliked him. As distinguished a representative as Joaquim José Pacheco could exclaim in the Brazilian Chamber of Deputies in the mid-nineteenth century: "What is shameful is to fawn upon the foreigner! Let us unite against the foreigner!"⁹ Yet at the same time, there was almost an obsession to please the foreigner, to receive his approbation. Mouthing anti-foreign phrases, the Brazilians—particularly the elite—slavishly copied European styles, words, customs, and tastes, especially those of France and England. The diplomat and novelist Gilberto Amado has given an accurate and jocular description of this aping of the foreigner in late nineteenth-century Brazil:

> At that time . . . Brazil did not manufacture a yard of silk, a shoe, a spool of thread; everything was imported. The names on the packing boxes were indecipherable to me. . . . Men's clothing for a tropical climate was made of English cloth suitable for life in the unheated homes of an English winter. I asked myself: how did they stand the heat? The ladies, when they took off their shoes at home, used slippers of heavy wool as if they were in Siberia. Years later I saw, in Rio, Quintino Bocaiúva, at the door of Watson's on the corner of Rua do Ouvidor, dressed in a frock coat of heavy material and wearing gloves. When I look at a photograph of José do Patrocínio, I note the collar of twill, and I ask myself how he could stand, during the abolitionist campaign, to give his speeches in the Recreio Dramático with that pressure on his body. Imagining the rivers of sweat pouring down, I sweat with him. In Pernambuco, we students of the Faculty wore morning coats and riding coats. In Rosa dos Alpes, a shop of Castro Alves, I saw at the door a well-known doctor, Artur Costa, with a glistening top hat just like those I later saw in Europe during the winter. Senator Rosa e Silva also went around in a top hat. Aníbal Freire never arrived at the office of the *Diário de Pernambuco* without his morning coat and top hat. How did we put up with that? Everything came from abroad. . . . Except for the poor, I never saw in the Pernambuco of my time anyone dressed in light clothing.¹⁰

Amado chose his examples well. They are amusing. They are also scornful, which is precisely what their author intended them to be. They reveal the frustrations and lack of confidence felt by Brazilians in the nineteenth century, tendencies that inhibited the full development of nationalism.

Those chiefly concerned with nationalism in the nineteenth century were the urban elite, who were located mainly in the three bustling ports of the realm—Recife, Bahia, and Rio de Janeiro. From their ranks came the writers, many of the politicians, the newspaper editors, and the orators who would stir the national soul. More often than not, they were the ones who directly confronted the foreigners. Occasionally, they took their case to the people, and the streets of Recife and Rio de Janeiro more than once echoed with xenophobic cries. Generally, however, the intellectuals chose to discuss, debate, and plan their country's future in the relative tranquillity of the coffee shops, book stores, and *salons*. Although they made some important contributions to the development of Brazilian nationalism, they were more successful in pointing out the factors that inhibited the development of Brazil than they were in defining the course the nation should follow.

Representative of the nationalists during the first decades of the empire was José Bonifácio de Andrada e Silva, known as the Patriarch of Brazilian Independence for his vital role in encouraging Pedro to sever relations with Portugal. Bonifácio warned the new nation against foreign influences and called for a strengthening of traditional Brazilian customs. He was particularly concerned about the threat to the nation posed by racial division. He proposed the gradual emancipation of the slaves, and the assimilation of Negroes and Indians into the national family. Bonifácio also favored a project that would kindle nationalist emotions for many generations: the removal of the nation's capital from the coast, and its close ties with Europe, to the Brazilian interior. In short, he wanted a Brazil that would not be a blind imitation of Europe but a true reflection of its own past and environment.

One of the most articulate sponsors of early Brazilian na-

tionalism was the Instituto Histórico e Geográfico Brasileiro
(Brazilian Geographical and Historical Institute), established
in Rio de Janeiro in 1838. Its founders sought to increase national pride through fostering a better knowledge of the nation. The Institute's Secretary, Januário da Cunha Barbosa,
stated the group's purpose: "We are going to save from the
unmerited obscurity in which they lie today many facts about
the history of our country and the lives of its most worthy
sons; we are going to ascertain with the greatest possible
accuracy the exact location of our most notable cities and
towns, the courses of our abundant rivers, the area of our
lands, the configuration of our mountains and the capacity
of our innumerable ports."[11] Through its periodical, the *Revista do Instituto Histórico e Geográfico Brasileiro*, the Institute undertook a campaign to glorify all things Brazilian.
In their praise of Brazil's past and their optimism about its
future, the early issues of the review read like pages from
the writings of the eighteenth-century nativists—of whom, in
truth, they were the successors. In the first issue of the review, Cunha Barbosa rhapsodized about "the riches of [Bra-
zil's] mines and forests, the products of its fields and hills,
the extent of its rivers and bays, the variety and ostentation
of its vegetation, the abundance and precocity of its fruits,
the surprising novelty of its animals, and, finally, the constant
benignity of its climate."[12] Cunha Barbosa only reflected the
will of his *confrères* when he evoked Rocha Pita as the spiritual mentor of the fledgling Institute.[13] The President of the
Institute, Visconde de São Leopoldo, continued in the same
vein in the second issue:

> Brazil lies beneath a benign and friendly sky, displaying an
> earth pierced here and there by ranges of mountains of varied
> configurations, some crowned with bald peaks that break
> through the clouds, others capped by dense, green forests,
> pouring forth their streams of bubbling water; this awesome
> majesty contrasts with the calm green of the cultivated valleys

and in our flatter provinces with the plowed fields which appear like ocean waves suddenly made motionless. Here everything pleases or astounds. A great variety of views and sensations banishes all tedious monotony. Brazil is located at the most advantageous geographical spot in the world for commerce, with excellent ports on the ocean, great lakes, or rather landlocked seas, and navigable rivers of enormous extent. Our developing agriculture and industry will attract to our shores the representatives of the advanced and cultivated nations who in search of the profits of commerce will bring us civilization; the foreigner, so given to the sciences, will come to this virgin soil to study nature and to drink deeply of her inspiration. . . . Everything points to the fact that Brazil is destined to be not accidentally, but by necessity, a center of enlightenment and civilization and an arbiter of the politics of the New World.[14]

The nationalists in the Institute did not look kindly upon the foreigners engaged in writing the history of Brazil. During the first half of the century, a number of non-Brazilians had produced solid historical works. Andrew Grant, Robert Southey, and John Armitage of Great Britain, and Jean Ferdinand Denis of France, were the most outstanding. The fact that they had been far more successful than the natives in writing Brazilian history prompted Cunha Barbosa to ask caustically: "Are we always going to leave the writing of our history to the snooping genius of the foreigners, who do not possess that fitting discernment which a national author would?"[15] Because of such nationalistic attitudes, the best of the foreign-written histories, Southey's three-volume *History of Brazil*, received a cool welcome. That massive work by a Protestant foreigner aroused more suspicion than approval. Although Brazilians for some decades plagiarized freely and extensively from it, it exerted little influence on the official policy of the Institute, which preferred to follow the path marked by Rocha Pita: to praise rather than to examine critically.

Yet it was a foreigner, Karl Friedrich Philipp von Martius, who discovered an important key to the interpretation and

understanding of Brazil. The German scientist had spent the
years 1817–20 traveling through the country to gather botan-
ical specimens. Two decades later, when the Institute sponsored a contest to solicit answers to the question of how the
history of Brazil might best be written, Martius submitted a
penetrating essay that displayed a remarkably clear vision
of the uniqueness of Brazil. He saw the amalgamation of the
three races, and their contributions to a single civilization, as
the salient Brazilian theme:

> Anyone who undertakes to write the history of Brazil, a country
> which promises so much, should never lose sight of the ele-
> ments which contributed to the development of man. These
> diverse elements come from the three races, namely: the cop-
> per-colored or the American, the white or the Caucasian, and
> the black or the Ethiopian. Because of the mutual and chang-
> ing relations of the three races, the present-day population
> consists of a novel mixture whose history therefore has a very
> particular stamp. . . .
>   Each physical and moral peculiarity characterizing the dif-
> ferent races offers a special force in this development of a new
> people. The more energy, number, and dignity characterize the
> race, the greater will be its influence on the common develop-
> ment. Thus it necessarily follows that the Portuguese, as the
> discoverer, conqueror, and master, greatly influenced this de-
> velopment; and because the Portuguese created the conditions
> and the physical and moral guarantees for an independent
> kingdom, they emerge as the most powerful and vital force.
> However, it certainly would be a great error for the principles
> of a pragmatic historiography if we disregarded the force of
> the natives and the imported Negroes, who likewise contributed
> to the physical, moral, and civic development of the whole
> population. The natives as well as the Negroes resisted the
> dominant race. . . .
>   We will never be permitted to doubt that providential will
> predestined this mixture for Brazil. The powerful river of Por-
> tuguese blood ought to absorb the small tributaries of the In-
> dian and Ethiopian races. . . . Thus I consider the Brazilians'
> personal relations, which allow the Negro and the Indian to
> influence the development of the Brazilian nationality, to be

designated for the destiny of the country. . . . The reflective historian's essential task should be to show that the conditions were established during Brazil's development for the improving of the three races, which are placed next to each other in a manner previously unknown in history, and that they should help each other in every way.[16]

In most respects, Martius' views were too advanced for his day. Although the essay received the first prize from the Institute, no one seriously followed the suggested plan for nearly a century—not until Gilberto Freyre took up the theme of racial amalgamation in his brilliant study *Casa Grande e Senzala* (*The Masters and the Slaves*), published in 1934. Much more in accordance with the immediate objectives of the Institute was Martius' reminder of the role the study of history could play in encouraging the growth of national feelings: "History is the master of the present and the future. It can spread noble, patriotic sentiments among contemporaries. A history of Brazil ought to stimulate love of country, courage, constancy, industry, fidelity, prudence, in a word, all the civic virtues in its Brazilian readers."[17] The Institute hoped to do just that, but it held no monopoly of the nationalism of the urban intellects.

The nineteenth-century Brazilian novelists generally followed the style of the European masters, but a few of them displayed nationalistic tendencies in their works. One of the earliest Brazilian novels, *Memórias de um Sargento de Milícias* (Memoirs of a Militia Sergeant) (1854–55), by Manoel Antônio de Almeida, drew wholly upon national themes. The author not only vividly described the *carioca* (Rio de Janeiro) scene, he liberally employed local expressions and words. His contributions to nationalism were subtle, probably unconscious. That was not true of many of the literary figures of the empire. Raul Pompéia, for example, whose suicide in 1895 at the age of thirty-two deprived Brazil of a gifted novelist, advised that "in order to save itself as a Nation, as a Fatherland, Brazil needs to adopt a policy of nationalism. It is not only commerce which lacks that fundamental doctrine, it is necessary also to make nationalism a part of the education of the young and to strengthen in their tender minds respect for Brazilian civic affairs by teaching them national history and patriotic hymns."[18]

As they searched the Brazilian past and surroundings for suitable subjects, the literati eventually turned their attention to a feature of Brazilian life not found in Europe: the Indian, and, in particular, the widely scattered Tupi, the largest and most important group. The exact position of the Indian in Brazilian civilization had never been satisfactorily resolved. His contributions to that civilization were many. Basically, he taught the European to adapt to the new land. His reward was enslavement, despite the best intentions of crown and church. Both institutions had sought to protect the Indian and to guarantee him a place within the empire. But their efforts were thwarted by the planters, who desperately needed laborers. Those Indians whom unaccustomed labor and disease did not kill either fled deeper and deeper into the interior or mixed their blood with that of the Europeans or, to a lesser extent, of the Africans. By the nineteenth century, the Indian was a pathetic remnant of his former self.

Yet, although the Indian as an individual was scorned, as a symbol he was cherished. He came to represent the original Brazil before the coming of the detested Portuguese. After independence, Brazilians pointed with pride to any trace of Indian blood in their veins, and many of them exchanged their Portuguese names for Indian ones. The Visconde de Jequitinhonha was a perfect example of that trend. Born Francisco Gomes Brandão, he took the Indian name Francisco Je Acaiaba Montezuma before his elevation to the nobility.

The full tide of nineteenth-century Indianism swept in between the years 1840 and 1875. During those years, poets such as Gonçalves Dias, in his *Poesias Americanas* (American Poems), and novelists, of whom the foremost representative was José de Alencar, exalted the Indian over the Portuguese. Alencar advised his fellow intellectuals that "the knowledge of the Indian language [Tupi] is the basis for a national literature."[19] Brazil's first outstanding historian in the national period, Francisco Adolfo de Varnhagen, concurred: "For Brazilian literature, the ancient language of our land [Tupi] is much more important than the study of Greek or other academic languages."[20]

Alencar, the most prolific and masterful contributor to the movement to glorify the Indian, wrote four Indianist novels: *O Guarani, Iracema, Ubirajara,* and *As Minas de Prata* (The Silver Mines). The most influential of these, *O Guarani,* was a complete idealization of the Indian. Peri, the Indian hero, was strong, honorable, and courageous; he stood out in sharp contrast to the more slippery Portuguese characters in the novel. The Brazilians saw in Peri the very qualities —pride, honor, and independence—that they valued in themselves, and the novel quickly became very popular.

The *Revista do Instituto Histórico e Geográfico Brasileiro* also frequently featured essays on the Indian past. The authors condemned the treatment of the Indians by the early Portuguese colonists, who they believed had debased the only "real" Brazilians. It was an emotional condemnation clouded by their hatred of the Portuguese. The remembrance of the Indian past was an important step toward the creation and recognition of a national culture.

Artists and composers also incorporated Indian and Brazilian themes into their works. The composer Carlos Gomes chose Alencar's *O Guarani* as the basis for an opera of the same name. His music was decidedly Italian but his plot was Brazilian. *O Guarani* remains the major national opera; its rousing overture has become as familiar to Brazilians as their national anthem. The composers Alexandre Levy and Alberto Nepomuceno experimented with Brazilian folk music in an effort to give their compositions the "sound" of Brazil. Among the painters, Pedro Américo and Vítor Meirelles chose subjects out of the Brazilian past for their vast historical canvases.

The use of the Indian theme was the major effort on the part of the nationalists to create a positive national culture. By and large, however, instead of searching for national values, the intellectuals continued to condemn the false Brazilian culture imported from Europe. In the last decades of the Second Empire, new voices spoke out to decry the cultural unreality. One of the most effective young nationalists to take the role of devil's advocate was the literary critic Sílvio Romero, who began to publish in 1871. Romero warned that all too often Brazilians looked abroad for their inspiration, thereby missing material of local importance. He aimed his critical barbs at "the figure of the imitator, of the slavish and witless copier of each and every trifle that the ships from Portugal or France or any other place bring us."[21] Brazilian literature should have its roots in the people and interpret the national environment, traditions, and sentiments. Romero crusaded indefatigably for the creation of a national literature. The major obstacle, he informed his compatriots, was that "we do not know ourselves."[22] Romero was one of the most important of the nineteenth-century intellectuals to advocate national introspection.

Another young scholar and critic to appear on the national scene during the 1870's was João Capistrano de Abreu. Capistrano protested, in much the same vein as Romero, that Brazilian art, music, and literature were not expressive of the national soul. Brazilian culture was only a faint shadow of European culture. It had little or nothing to do with its surroundings. In short, it did not represent "the conscious expression of the people."[23] Both Capistrano and Romero arrived at the unhappy conclusion that Brazilian culture was neither natural, original, nor indigenous. Their criticism cleared the ground for a more native culture to flourish on Brazilian soil.

Until 1889, Brazilian national sentiment had a convenient focal point: the throne of the emperor, which commanded the loyalty of all regions and classes. As the center of an enormous, sprawling, and disconnected empire, the monarchy contributed greatly to Brazilian unity and continuity. Its force and influence guaranteed a strength, stability, and tranquillity not found in Spanish-speaking South America, which had splintered into nine nations from two viceroyalties. Conclusive proof of the throne's centripetal powers was shown in 1840, when Pedro II ascended the throne. The empire had been torn asunder by a series of bloody provincial rebellions during the Regency of 1831–40. The long Second Empire (1840–89) welded the nation together again. Brazilians, who had rejected Pedro I because he was Portuguese, embraced the Brazilian-born Pedro II, and the growing nationalism evident during his reign countered and quieted the threatening regionalism.

Brazil changed greatly during the Second Empire. Much of that change was due to the growing prosperity of the new coffee industry, which by the mid-nineteenth century had replaced the sugar industry as the backbone of the economy. The earnings from coffee exports were invested in local industry, railroads, and the renovation of ports. The telegraph, submarine cable, and steamships brought the nation closer together and put Brazil in increasingly rapid communication with Europe.

A major catalyst of change was the long War of the Triple Alliance (1865–70). In late 1864, Paraguay, fearful of Brazil's intentions in the Plata area, invaded the province of Mato Grosso and attacked Rio Grande do Sul. The ensuing war tested the strength, unity, and sense of purpose of the empire. Pedro II referred to the war as "a good electric shock to nationality." But the prolonged campaign also brought many crises in its wake. The financial burden weighed heavily. A ministerial crisis in 1868 returned the Conservatives to power, and, as a result, the more radical of the Liberals began to flirt with federalist ideas. In 1870, the newly formed Republican Party, which drew its membership largely from the cities, issued a manifesto calling for the establishment of a federal republic. The fall of Napoleon III was also felt in Brazil and helped the cause of the republicans. Many soldiers had been exposed to republican institutions and ideology during their years at the front, and they too returned home eager for change. Positivist philosophy became the rage among many intellectuals. The movements for the abolition of slavery and for the separation of church and state grew in size and influence.

The monarchy showed itself to be increasingly out of touch with the changing times. It did not represent the emerging middle class, the coffee interests, or the new commercial and industrial elements. Furthermore, it managed to alienate even its stanchest supporters. Church officials quarreled with the Emperor and consequently became cool toward the monarchy. The emancipation of the slaves in 1888, without indemnification for the owners, aroused the opposition of the sugar aristocracy and the more conservative elements of the coffee class.

The military, which had become a well-established institution in Brazil as a result of the war against Paraguay, felt neglected by the Emperor, who showed little interest in military affairs. With few duties to distract them, the officers also became increasingly preoccupied with questions of prestige and honor, and small incidents between imperial and military authorities broke out in the years after 1879.

Aware of the mounting dissatisfaction among the officers, the republicans decided to exploit it to their own advantage.

The idealistic young officers, concerned less with questions of military honor than with problems of national development, listened attentively to both republican and positivist propaganda. The military school in Rio de Janeiro reverberated with discussions of republican ideology; in the popular classes of Colonel Benjamin Constant de Magalhães, the cadets heard enthusiastic lectures on positivism. These young officers reflected the widening breach between the middle class from which they came and the imperial government. But unlike the urban middle class—or any other group in Brazil, for that matter—they had both the organization and the power to effect change. The republicans understood that the military held the key that would unlock the door to the republic, but they realized that the support of the junior officers was meaningless without the cooperation of their seniors. In the late 1880's, the ranking officers began to move toward the republican camp as the logical alternative to supporting an empire which they felt mistreated or neglected them. When the most powerful figure in the army, Marshal Deodoro da Fonseca, became convinced of the validity of the republican cause, the fate of the monarchy was sealed. The Marshal commanded the loyalty of the entire armed forces, and with him they turned on the empire.

On November 15, 1889, the army, under Deodoro da Fonseca, marched against the royal palace and occupied the principal government buildings in Rio de Janeiro. The Marshal informed a surprised nation of the action taken by the armed forces in the name of the people. The Brazilians generally acquiesced in the change. Of the provinces, only Maranhão and Bahia offered some token protest or resistance. The general tranquillity seemed to bear witness to the structural weakness and lack of vitality of the empire; it would appear that the military had simply delivered the *coup de grâce*.

The aged Emperor sailed into European exile, leaving the

new republic in the hands of the military. The military also fell heir to the emperor's role as the unifying force in the country; indeed, at that time, it was the only institution that was national in scope and prepared to play such a role.[24] The officers took their new assignment seriously; it would prove impossible thereafter to divest them of it. They kept direct control of the government until 1894, when they turned over the presidency to a civilian and retired to the wings, from which they studiously observed and occasionally prompted. They noted with pleasure the increase in nationalism under the republic.

4. The New Brazil and the Foundations of Twentieth-Century Nationalism

The establishment of the new republic* marked the opening of an era of self-confidence in Brazil. Brazilians had considerable reason to be confident. The last half of the nineteenth century had witnessed a profound alteration of the centuries-old institutional structures as well as gratifying material progress. The principal export, coffee, continued to sell well abroad. One result of the prosperity was the shift of the economic center of the nation from the sugar-producing Northeast to the coffee-producing Southeast. Political power shifted accordingly to the more liberal and progressive Southeast, the center of support for the emancipation of the slaves and the establishment of the republic. The vigorous and aggressive coffee planters replaced the sugar barons, who for centuries had dominated the nation's economic, political, and social life.

By 1890, the population of Brazil totaled approximately 14 million persons. At the top of the social ladder were the wealthy plantation owners and their families, who numbered around 300,000; at the bottom were the 600,000 Negroes recently freed from slavery. In between stood the wage-earning farm hands, the small and medium-sized farmers, the mechanics and artisans, the shopkeepers, the government employees, the military, the merchants, and the intellectuals. A new element in Brazilian society was the increasing num-

* Known in Brazilian history as the Old Republic (1889–1930).

ber of European immigrants, principally from Italy, Portugal, Spain, and Germany, who settled in the Southeast. Their European ideas inevitably helped to modify and liberalize the thinking of the area. For the first time it was possible to speak of a Brazilian middle class, whose most informed and vocal element was to be found in the cities.

Brazil was clearly becoming more urbanized. Santos emerged as the world's major coffee port; São Paulo, whose population jumped from 35,000 in 1883 to half a million in 1918, was rapidly developing into a dynamic financial and manufacturing center; Rio de Janeiro was completely renovated. Manaus, giddy with rubber riches, was transformed from a small village into a cosmopolitan city with a splendid opera house, sidewalk cafés, electrically illuminated streets, and a bustling stock exchange. The Mineiros built a sparkling new capital city, Belo Horizonte. Roads and railroads were built to connect the major cities of the South and were extended inland to reach previously untapped markets and resources. The number of new businesses multiplied annually.

The early decades of the republic also saw the successful achievement of one of the principal national goals: the definitive delineation of the national frontiers. The skillful Luso-Brazilian diplomacy of the eighteenth century, and the able imperial diplomats, had laid the necessary groundwork. The new republic called from the obscurity of a minor diplomatic post a scholarly aristocrat, the Baron of Rio-Branco, to defend Brazil's territorial claims at the conference table. A dedicated nationalist, Rio-Branco pushed those claims to the limit. From 1895 to 1909, he won a series of diplomatic victories based on the principle of *uti possidetis*. He triumphed over Brazil's archrival, Argentina, when President Grover Cleveland made the Missões arbitral award in 1895. Five years later, the Baron again emerged successful from an arbitration court, this time defeating a major European power, France, and allowing Brazil to assert its sovereignty over the territory between the Amazon and Oiapoque rivers. The "Golden Chancellor" won the Acre territory from Bolivia in 1903, and in 1909 favorably settled Brazil's territorial dispute with Peru. During an extraordinary career, he delineated approximately 9,000 miles of frontier and added nearly 115,000 square miles to the national domain without the need for one Brazilian soldier to fire a shot. His victories raised him to the status of a hero; they also raised Brazil's diplomatic vision from its borders to the world beyond.

Having defended Brazil's borders successfully, Rio-Branco channeled his and the nation's energy into a new and more aggressive policy. That new direction was well illustrated by Brazil's attitude toward the two Hague Peace Conferences. In 1899, only Brazil and Mexico among the Latin American nations received invitations to attend the First Hague Conference. Mexico accepted but Brazil declined, on the grounds that nothing of national interest would be discussed. In 1907, Brazil not only eagerly accepted an invitation to the Second Hague Conference but requested an official position for its principal representative and dispatched one of the largest delegations to the gathering (larger than that of the United States, for example). Only eight years separated the two conferences, yet Brazil's attitudes toward them were entirely different.

Under Rio-Branco's skillful guidance, Brazil's international prestige soared. Rio de Janeiro boasted the largest number of foreign legations of all the South American capitals; in 1905, Brazil exchanged ambassadors with Washington, the first and for a long time the only South American country to do so. Elihu Root made the first visit abroad by a United States Secretary of State when he traveled to Brazil in 1906. A series of distinguished foreigners, including Georges Clémenceau, William Jennings Bryan, James Bryce, and Sarah Bernhardt, visited Brazil. The Vatican selected a Brazilian bishop as the first Latin American cardinal. Foreign naval squadrons and special diplomatic missions arrived to pay their respects. Little wonder, then, that Rio-Branco's policies enjoyed popularity throughout the republic. They were supported by citizens of all political persuasions and were seen as the expression of a unified nation. The Baron's successes contributed significantly to Brazil's self-assurance.

Brazilian literature also entered a golden age under the new republic. Poets such as Olavo Bilac and Raymundo Correia wrote verses of rare beauty and depth. Some of the finest novelists Brazil has seen—Machado de Assis, Lima Barreto, and Graça Aranha—were publishing. And in 1902, Euclides da Cunha's *Os Sertões* burst on the literary firmament.

As a result of peace, prosperity, and material and spiritual progress, Brazilian nationalism began to shed those defensive characteristics it had assumed during the nineteenth century. Nationalism became less a series of isolated and erratic reactions to outside stimuli and more a philosophic impulse to develop the nation, to define the national character, and to project a favorable image abroad. In short, an aggressive or constructive nationalism was forming.

The intellectuals contributed generously to the invigorated nationalist movement. More than anyone else, they dressed the stage for the drama of twentieth-century nationalism. Eventually, their activities spilled over into the political field, as they joined or founded political movements to implement their concept of nationalism and to agitate for change.

The century opened with the publication of Afonso Celso's blatantly chauvinistic *Porque Me Ufano do Meu País* (Why I Am Proud of My Country). In this exaggerated, simplistic, and often erroneous book, Celso sang a hymn of praise to the past. He pointed with pride to the vast size, beauty, and natural wealth of Brazil. He commented on the excellent qualities of the Brazilian—his friendliness and valor—and the glorious events in Brazil's history. Celso sought to arouse a love for the fatherland by emphasizing its natural advantages and achievements, and thus to combat a prevalent belief of the times that the Brazilian and his civilization were inferior. (The author later defended himself from critics on the grounds that, in the matter of patriotism, excessive enthusiasm was to be preferred to a deficiency of it.) The book so pleased the nationalists that, since its publication in 1901, it has gone through fourteen editions. Celso had great faith in nationalism as a force: "The spirit of nationalism is the incalculable dynamo of energy of our times; it is the lever which moves the world."[1]

Other intellectuals of the period made contributions of a more serious and scholarly nature to the understanding of Brazil. One of the most significant of these was made by the historian João Capistrano de Abreu, who raised Brazilian historical studies to a new level of sophistication. Capistrano de Abreu was the first to point out the influence of the interior and of the Indian on the formation of Brazil. He presented his thesis in 1889 in a short but brilliant essay, "Os Caminhos Antigos e o Povoamento do Brasil" ("Old Roads and the Populating of Brazil"), which José Honório Rodrigues has compared favorably in content and influence to Frederick Jackson Turner's *The Frontier in American History*.[2] According to Capistrano, the interior was the true Brazil; the heavily populated coast was merely an extension of Europe. Only when the coastal inhabitants turned their backs on the sea and penetrated the interior did they shed their European ways and become Brazilianized. Capistrano's disciple Afonso de Taunay elaborated on those ideas in exhaustive studies of *bandeirante* movements in the *sertão*.[3]

Further confirmation of Capistrano's thesis came from the penetrating analysis by Euclides da Cunha, who, in his masterpiece, *Os Sertões* (translated into English as *Rebellion in the Backlands*), published in 1902, proved himself one of Brazil's most gifted writers. As a journalist, da Cunha had accompanied the federal army into the *sertão* of Bahia on its mission to wipe out the defiant backwoods followers of the religious mystic Antônio Conselheiro. The different people, customs, topography, even the differently spoken language, astounded da Cunha. He felt that he had been transported "outside Brazil." Accustomed to life along the coast, he was unprepared for what he saw in the interior. The existence of "two societies," one quite distinct from the other, within a single nation left a lasting impression on him: "Here was an absolute and radical break between the coastal cities and the clay huts of the interior, one that so disturbed the rhythm of our evolutionary development and which was so deplorable a stumbling block to national unity."[4] He concluded that what he beheld in the interior was the real Brazil. He spoke of the backwoodsmen as "the very core of our nationality, the bedrock of our race," and of their society as "the vigorous core of our national life."[5] Some years later, after much reflection, he reinforced these conclusions:

I did encounter in the backlands type [*sertanejo*] an ethnic subcategory already formed and one which, as a result of historical conditions, had been freed of the exigencies of a borrowed civilization such as would have hindered its definitive evolution. This is equivalent to saying that in that indefinable compound—the Brazilian—I came upon something that was stable, a point of resistance reminiscent of the integrating molecule in the initial stage of crystallizations. And it was natural enough that, once having admitted the bold and inspiring conjecture that we are destined to national unity, I should have seen in those sturdy *caboclos* the hardy nucleus of our future, the bedrock of our race. . . .

As we make our way deeper into the land . . . the pure white, the pure Negro, and the pure Indian are now a rarity. The generalized miscegenation, meanwhile, has given rise to every variety of racial crossing; but, as we continue on our way, these shadings tend to disappear, and there is to be seen a greater uniformity of physical and moral characteristics. In brief, we have struck bedrock—in the man of the backlands.[6]

The publication of *Os Sertões* created a sensation. It has since become a Brazilian classic.

The Indians continued to attract the attention of the intelligentsia. But in the twentieth century, the romantic notions with which the mid-nineteenth century literati had regarded the Indian gave way to more serious efforts to understand the aboriginal cultures. In 1876, Couto de Magalhães published his study of Tupi legends, *O Selvagem* (The Savage), and in 1890 João Barbosa Rodrigues published another, *Poranduba Amazonense* (Amazon Tales). The works of those two authors marked the transition from the heyday of the romantic Indianist movement to the early twentieth-century interest in the Indian.

In 1900, the prose and poetry of one of Brazil's best-known Indianist writers, Alexandre José de Melo Moraes Filho, were published in a single volume under the title *Pátria Selvagem* (Untamed Land). The short stories of Alberto Rangel, published in 1907 as *Inferno Verde* (Green Hell), Salvador de Mendonça's poem "João Caboclo" (1910), and the poems of Humberto de Campos, *Poeira* (Dust) (1911), reflected sadly on the fate of the Indian. Clearly in a masochistic mood, the Brazilians flagelated themselves for their mistreatment of the Indian.

In 1910, the Indian Protection Service was founded, under the direction of General Cândido Rondon, himself part Indian, to protect the remaining Indians and to attempt to incorporate them into the Brazilian family. Some nationalists promoted a movement to replace the Portuguese language with the dominant Indian language in Brazil, Tupi. The Partido Republicano Feminino (Women's Republican Party), whose leaders dressed in Indian costumes, campaigned for the obligatory teaching of Tupi in the schools.

This revived interest in the Indian was matched by a similar search for the roots of popular culture. Writers turned their attention to the rich folklore of their native land, and began to record and study the customs and tales of the people. Sílvio Romero made an early contribution to the nation's awareness of its popular culture in two anthologies of folk poems and songs, *Contos Populares do Brasil* (Brazilian Folk Tales), first published in 1885, and *Estudos sôbre a Poesia Popular do Brasil* (Studies of Brazilian Folk Poetry), published in 1888. Those anthologies, and their introductory essays, revealed more about Romero than they did about the nature and value of Brazilian folklore. Yet they were an important beginning for the broader and more profound studies that followed in the twentieth century.

The turn of the century witnessed the publication of a number of studies by Alexandre José de Melo Moraes Filho, who made a significant contribution to the knowledge of popular customs in Brazil. Of particular interest were his *Festas e Tradições Populares do Brasil* (Folk Festivals and Traditions in Brazil), and *História e Costumes* (History and Customs). The latter work included detailed descriptions of the observances of Christmas, New Year's, and the Day of the Three Kings in Bahia; St. John's Day celebrations in Sergipe; and the fishermen's festival in Rio de Janeiro. In 1908, Francisco Augusto Pereira da Costa published his classic study of regional folkways, *Folclore Pernambucano* (Pernambucan Folklore), a valuable guide to the folk poetry, superstitions, and legends of the Northeast.

The studies of the indigenous and popular cultures introduced new words and expressions to the literati, who timidly adopted some of them. One of the earliest writers to accept the new themes and styles was the novelist Lima Barreto, who delighted in firing broadsides against the traditional Portuguese literary patterns. An energetic iconoclast, he tumbled many literary idols. Barreto also enjoyed exposing the foibles of the urban dweller in Brazil. He even chose to look at the humorous side of nationalism. In his brilliant novel *Triste Fim de Policarpo Quaresma* (The Sad End of Policarpo

Quaresma), published in 1911, he poked fun at the nationalists through the meticulously drawn picture of his hero—or
anti-hero—a devoted nationalist.

> Policarpo was a patriot. Since his childhood, some twenty years
> back, his love for his Fatherland consumed him. It was not the
> ordinary type of love, verbal and vacant; it was a serious senti-
> ment, grave and absorbing. He had no political ambitions.
> What he sought, or better what his patriotism caused him to
> seek, was a complete knowledge of Brazil, making him medi-
> tate on its resources so that later he could point out remedies
> and progressive measures with full knowledge of the reasons
> for national ills.
>
> He did not tell where he was born. Certainly it was not in
> São Paulo, nor in Rio Grande do Sul, nor in Pará. Whoever
> tried to find some regionalism in this man would err. Above
> all else, Quaresma was a Brazilian. He had no predilection for
> this or that part of his country, what made him vibrate with
> passion was not the pampas of the south with their cattle, nor
> the coffee of São Paulo, nor the gold and diamonds of Minas
> Gerais, nor the beauty of Guanabara, nor the majesty of the
> Paulo Afonso Falls, nor the poetic inspiration of Gonçalves
> Dias, nor the impelling force of Andrade Neves, it was all of
> these together, united and enfolded in the star-studded flag
> of the Southern Cross. . . .
>
> He studied, but he studied the Fatherland, its natural
> riches, history, geography, literature, and politics. Quaresma
> knew all the animals, vegetables, and minerals that Brazil pos-
> sessed. He knew the value of the diamonds and gold exported
> from Minas Gerais, the war of liberation from the Dutch, the
> battles of the Paraguayan war, the sources and courses of all
> the rivers. He defended peevishly and passionately the preemi-
> nence of the Amazon over all rivers in the rest of the world. In
> order to do that he even resorted to the crime of subtracting a
> few miles from the Nile, and it was with this rival of "his" river
> that he was most in conflict. Woe to him who cited the Nile
> first! In general calm and collected, the major became agitated
> and acrimonious when discussing the length of the Amazon and
> the Nile. . . .
>
> There was one year when he dedicated himself to the study
> of the Tupi language. Each morning from dawn to lunch he

grappled with Montoya's *Grammar and Dictionary of the Tupi Language,* which he studied with dedication and perseverance. At his office in the armory, the petty clerks, secretaries, and office boys, hearing of his pursuit of the Tupi tongue, started calling him—without knowing its exact origin—Ubirajara. Once the clerk Azevedo, a bit distracted and without suspecting who stood behind him, remarked in a loud voice, "Have you noticed that today Ubirajara is late?"

Now, Quaresma was well respected in the armory. His age, learning, modesty, and honesty won the respect of all. Sensing that the nickname applied to him, he did not lose his dignity in an outbreak of insults and vituperation. He straightened up, adjusted his pince-nez, raised his index finger and responded, "Mr. Azevedo do not be flippant. Do not ridicule those who labor in silence for the glory and emancipation of the Fatherland." . . .

That day when he was called Ubirajara to his face, Quaresma remained reserved, silent, and taciturn. He spoke only once, when he went to wash his hands before the end of the day, at which time he overheard someone sigh, "Oh dear, when can I leave this place for Europe!" The major could not contain himself. He stared, adjusted his pince-nez, and spoke fraternally and persuasively, "Ingrate! You have the richest and most beautiful country and you yearn to visit others! For myself, if I could someday, I'd visit my own land from one end to the other."

The other objected, saying that here one encountered fevers and mosquitoes. The major responded with statistics and even proved exuberantly that the Amazon had one of the world's best climates.[7]

The studies and practices of the intellectuals in the early decades of the twentieth century indicated the mood prevalent among them: they frankly sought to break with the past. As if to symbolize the end of the era of bucolic nationalism, Menotti del Picchia bid farewell to the rural past in his poem *Juca Mulato,* the tale of the handsome *caboclo* who leaves the plantation for the city. Similarly, the intellectuals were turning from their praise of the country to their new occupation: to define and encourage the national culture. Elysio de

Carvalho boasted to his fellow intellectuals: "We are the descendants of a people of warriors, saints, heroes, and poets."[8] Imbued with such confidence, the intellectuals resolved to abandon their libraries and to take action.

Appropriately, that action reached its peak in 1922, during the centennial celebrations of independence. As "the nationalist movement agitated the country's soul from north to south,"[9] the young intellectuals presented their own manifesto of independence. They defined and enunciated the objectives of their Modernist movement during Modern Art Week, February 11–17, 1922, a celebration organized by a group of intellectuals in São Paulo. The week was inaugurated with a meeting at the São Paulo Municipal Theater. Graça Aranha, the highly respected author of *Canaan* and a member of the Brazilian Academy of Letters, opened the evening with a speech in which he proclaimed that the intellectuals were in rebellion against the stagnant state of the arts in Brazil. The young poets Guilherme de Almeida and Ronald de Carvalho read their verses, and the youthful Heitor Villa-Lobos conducted his own compositions, based on folk themes and employing indigenous instruments. Modern paintings and sculpture were displayed in the foyer of the theater. During the rest of the week, the young artists and intellectuals organized exhibitions, musical programs, poetry readings, and conferences to demonstrate not only new artistic trends, but a growing appreciation of the Brazilian environment. Their enthusiasm spread to other cities, and new nationalistic literary journals sprang up wherever the dedicated revolutionaries sowed their intellectual seeds.

The cries of the Modernists joined a larger chorus of voices throughout Latin America. In 1923, José Vasconcelos, Mexican Ambassador to Brazil and a leading intellectual and political figure, spoke of Latin America's struggle to achieve its own cultural identity when he unveiled a statue of Cuauhtémoc, a gift of the Mexican people to Brazil. Vasconcelos remarked that Cuauhtémoc, the last Aztec emperor, could be seen as the symbol of that struggle.

And now Cuauhtémoc is reborn because for our people the hour of our second independence, the independence of our civilization, the emancipation of our spirit—as a belated but inevitable corollary of our political emancipation—has struck. The first century of our national life has been a century of spiritual vassalage when we strove to be the perfect copy of the European; and this is the hour, not of regression, but most certainly of originality. . . . Tired, disgusted, of all this copied civilization . . . we interpret the vision of Cuauhtémoc as an anticipation of the . . . birth of the Latin American soul. . . . We wish to cease being Europe's spiritual colonies.[10]

The novelist Machado de Assis had earlier parodied the Brazilian's blind devotion to Europe in his novel *Dom Casmurro,* in which one of the novel's characters, José Dias, speaks of death as "going to the other Europe, the eternal one."[11] Such subservience to a foreign culture irked the nationalists, whose objective, in the words of Menotti del Picchia, was the "Brazilianization of Brazil."[12] "Let us forget the marble of the Acropolis and the towers of the Gothic cathedrals," exhorted Ronald de Carvalho, one of the leaders of the Modernist movement. "We are the sons of the hills and the forests. Stop thinking of Europe. Think of America."[13] The poet Carlos Drummond de Andrade expressed the same idea in his poem "Explicação":

It was my people and my land that made me the way I am,
And I am glad to have been born with this failing.
For me, the greatest of all follies is sighing for Europe.[14]

One of the most important ways of achieving cultural independence was to declare the nation's literary independence. "Brazil has to have a national literature," argued the young writer Sérgio Buarque de Holanda. "Inspiration from national sources, respect for traditions, and submission to the profound voices of our race will bring about this desired result."[15]

In a speech "The Modern Spirit," given on June 19, 1924, before the Brazilian Academy of Letters, Graça Aranha took the case directly to the citadel of literary traditionalism. He defended the national culture as a European legacy that had been transformed by the conditions of the New World. He accused the Academy of adhering too strictly to foreign literary traditions.

The nationalist writers boldly attacked the remaining stylistic conventions, which they regarded as restricting their own inventiveness. Vernacularisms appeared in writing and contributed significantly to the creation of a national literary style. Freedom of form, fresh images, a vigorous style, and originality of expression characterized the new literature. Above all, the literati declared and exercised their right to experiment. The concern with new styles and Brazilian themes meant that literature became increasingly national. The aims of the Modern Art Week triumphed and Brazilian literature —to use the words of Machado de Assis—"was dressing itself in the colors of the country."[16]

The Modernist movement also continued the efforts of the intelligentsia to define and explain their culture. Writers probed national psychology, questioned national motives, and re-examined the past.

The number of folkloric studies multiplied during the 1920's. Lindolfo Gomes enumerated the folkways of Minas Gerais in his *Contos Populares* (Folk Tales). João Simões Lopes, in *Cancioneiro Guasca, Coletânea de Poesia Popular Rio-grandense* (Southern Songbook: A Collection of Folk Poetry of Rio Grande do Sul) and *Contos Gauchescos e Lendas do Sul* (Gaucho Tales and Legends of the South), studied the popular culture of the southernmost part of Brazil. Gustavo Barroso made similar contributions to the knowledge of the Northeast in a variety of works, such as *Ao Som da*

Viola: Folclore (To the Strum of the Guitar: Folklore) and *Através dos Folclores* (Among Folkways). By the end of the 1920's, there was a respectable bibliography on the subject. Mário de Andrade, who emerged as the dean of the scholars in the field, initiated an active campaign to acquaint his compatriots with their culture and to urge his colleagues to study that invaluable source of information and inspiration. He also later set up courses in ethnography and folklore. Folklore also found its way into the national literature, as exemplified by Mário de Andrade's own novel, *Macunaíma,* published in 1928. Macunaíma, a Brazilian folk hero, has been called both the Peer Gynt and the Paul Bunyon of the tropics. The novel makes use of regionalisms and popular expressions, and its chief character synthesizes the qualities and the defects of the Brazilian "race."

A pessimistic analysis of Brazil, Paulo Prado's *Retrato do Brasil* (Portrait of Brazil), was also published in 1928. Prado's opening words—"In a radiant land live a sad people"—set the study's tone:

> Two tyrannical sentiments dominated Brazil: sensualism and a passion for gold. The history of Brazil is the disorderly development of those obsessions and the subjugation of the spirit and body of their victims. . . .
>
> In the pursuit of those desires—without any other ideal, or religion, or esthetics, or any political, intellectual, or artistic preoccupation—a sad race was created over the centuries.[17]

The history of Brazil, according to Prado, was the chaotic development of two passions, sensuality and greed.

Prado's outlook contrasted markedly with that expressed by Afonso Celso nearly three decades earlier. Yet Prado was no less nationalistic than Celso. He loved Brazil just as much, but he believed that only by diagnosing the weaknesses of the Brazilian character could corrections be made upon which future progress depended. Celso and Prado represent the two extreme views of Brazil—those of unbounded optimism and deep pessimism, a duality that is also found in the Brazilian character.

In 1934, the young sociologist Gilberto Freyre introduced a significant theme that would thereafter exercise a powerful influence on national thought. In his *The Masters and the Slaves,* Freyre expanded and popularized the idea of Martius that the uniqueness of the Brazilian civilization was the result of the contributions of three races. The effect of Freyre's great work was to free the literati from many of their cultural complexes and to make the African theme and miscegenation respectable. Miscegenation, it was at last realized, had made Brazil a homogeneous nation, despite its great size. Freyre's discussion of how a unique civilization had been created in Brazil opened up vast new areas of research and study.

Literature also welcomed the Negro. At the same time that Freyre was preparing his sociological study, Jorge de Lima was publishing poems on Negro themes. His works paid homage to the moral superiority of the Negro, in a manner reminiscent of the treatment earlier accorded the Indian. The Negro also began to appear as the protagonist in novels—not, as had frequently happened in the past, as a curiosity, but as a respected member of the community. Lins do Rego's *O Moleque Ricardo* (The Young Man Richard) and Jorge Amado's *Jubiabá,* both published in 1935, illustrated that trend.

In the years that followed, a number of other analytical studies of Brazil appeared. Among the most important were Plínio Salgado's *Psicologia da Revolução* (Psychology of Revolution); Sérgio Buarque de Holanda's *Raízes do Brasil* (The Roots of Brazil); Afonso Arinos de Melo Franco's *Introdução ao Estudo da Realidade Brasileira* (Introduction to the Study of the Brazilian Reality) and *Conceito da Civilização Brasileira* (Understanding Brazilian Civilization); and Freyre's *Brazil: An Interpretation,* which was first published in English and later translated into Portuguese.

In the second and third decades of the twentieth century, the intellectuals also formed movements to implement the goal boldly proclaimed by the Modernists—the Brazilianization of Brazil—and to popularize the ideas being supported in literary circles. Two such groups were the Verdamarelo and the Anta, led by Cassiano Ricardo and Plínio Salgado, among others. The very names of the groups revealed their nationalistic bent: the name "Verdamarelo" combines the Portuguese words for "green" and "yellow," the colors of the Brazilian flag; *anta* is the Indian name for the Brazilian tapir. Believing that the West was much more "Brazilian" than the coast, these groups drew their inspiration from the interior.

In his *Terra do Sol* (Land of the Sun), published in 1912, the nationalist Gustavo Barroso had lauded the virtues of the backlander—his strength, fortitude, honesty, simplicity, and perseverance—attributing them to the influence of the interior. Cassiano Ricardo further romanticized this view in his *Marcha para o Oeste* (March to the West), in which he contrasted the rustic democracy of the interior with the decadent feudalism of the coast. Like many intellectuals of his day, he believed that "the *bandeira* is not merely the most Brazilian historical episode. Besides having traced the geographic profile of Brazil, it is a social and political phenomenon which helps to clarify many of our present institutions."[18]

Other nationalist intellectual movements of the period sought to exalt the Indian and to glorify the native past. Two such groups were the pau-brasil and the Antropofagia, whose names also reveal their nationalistic inclinations. *Pau-brasil* (brazilwood) is the native tree that gave the country its name. Antropofagia refers to the Indians' cannibalistic tendencies. The adherents to the Antropofagia cause displayed a robust sense of humor too frequently lacking among the nationalists. For instance, they set the date of October 11, 1928, for the first World Conference of Antropofagia; as the day before Columbus Day, it marked the last day of "Free

America." They also proposed a calendar that would date from the day in 1556 when the Indians of Rio Grande do Norte killed and ate the first bishop of Brazil, Antônio Sardinha.

It soon became apparent that cultural nationalism had strong political undercurrents, for as Francisco de Assis Barbosa was later to observe, "It is impossible to separate literature from politics."[19] Many participants in the intellectual movements became deeply involved in politics in the decades of the 1920's and 1930's. They presented a wide spectrum of political preferences: Plínio Salgado became the leader of the fascist Integralist party, Oswald de Andrade flirted with Communism, Cassiano Ricardo and Menotti del Picchia favored the labor parties, Sérgio Milliet, Sérgio Buarque de Holanda, and Mário de Andrade, the democratic left.

The 1920's were indeed characterized by considerable political as well as cultural unrest. The restiveness was caused by a deepening disenchantment with the republic and a growing agitation for more effective, representative, and progressive government. The military reflected this dissatisfaction. On July 5, 1922, a small band of young officers staged an unsuccessful revolt at Fort Igrejinha in the Copacabana section of Rio de Janeiro. The young rebels, who represented a large proportion of the junior officers, had formulated no program beyond the desire to reform and modernize their country. Their goals were as idealistic as their planning was inept. Government forces promptly surrounded the fort, and the "Eighteen of Copacabana" emerged to fight it out on the Copacabana beach, where most of them lost their lives. One of the few survivors was Eduardo Gomes, who in the 1930's became a strong supporter of Getúlio Vargas. Two years later to the day, a second revolt of young officers broke out, this time in São Paulo. Their revolt touched off uprisings in Amazonas, Pará, Pernambuco, and Sergipe. Later in the year, violence erupted in Rio Grande do Sul. In the mid-1920's, the

youthful Luís Carlos Prestes organized disgruntled participants from the São Paulo and Rio Grande do Sul revolts into
a band of a thousand men. The "Prestes Column" marched
north from São Paulo to Maranhão, turned westward into the
interior, and finally disbanded at the Bolivian border after
a trek of 6,000 miles. That weird assortment of soldiers, officers, revolutionaries, and adventurers captured the imagination of the entire nation. The march became the symbol
of revolt against the unimaginative government in Rio de
Janeiro, which proved less and less capable of dealing with
the problems facing the nation.

There were few available avenues of protest. Political parties—which could have provided alternatives to the electorate
—were small and poorly organized. Ironically, although none
of them was national in scope, most of the political parties of
the Old Republic contained nationalistic planks in their plat-
forms. After World War I, the number of frankly nationalistic
parties multiplied; the majority were located in Rio de Janeiro and São Paulo. They were small, and their message sel-
dom extended beyond the confines of half a dozen coastal
cities. One of these parties was the Ação Social Nacionalista
(National Social Action, or ASN), based in Rio de Janeiro
and led by Afonso Celso. It is worth while outlining the program of the ASN, because it is typical of those of the other
Brazilian nationalist parties. The ASN advocated the transfer of the capital from the coast to the interior, the nationalization of commerce, retention of profits within the
country, nationalization of the press, creation of a national
theater, control of rents to limit foreign control of property,
establishment of agricultural credit, closer relations with the
other Latin American countries, and a stronger federal government. The proposal to relocate the federal capital in the
central highlands, "a perennial dream of Brazilian patriots,"[20]
symbolized their aspirations to "Brazilianize" Brazil. The desires to nationalize commerce and to control rents, and, to a

lesser degree, to nationalize the press, create a national theater, and keep profits within the country, reflected the Brazilians' continuing resentment of the resident Portuguese, who
still controlled a large share of domestic commerce. The ASN
program made no mention of industrialization or the preser-
vation of natural resources. Yet within a few years, industrialization and the nationalization of the oil industry would
be the major objectives of nationalist agitation. Nationalism
in the 1920's was still predominantly political and cultural
in its orientation.

That political nationalism could also assume profoundly
conservative tones was demonstrated by a Roman Catholic
movement that took shape during the 1920's. The aims of the
movement were defined in an editorial, signed by Father
Antônio Carmelo, that appeared in the monthly Catholic review *Brasilea:*

> I ought to make every effort to see that the Brazilians know
> each other intimately and love each other cordially and under-
> stand fully the secret of their national existence if they wish
> their nation to last forever robust, strong, and alert. I will not
> err if I tell them that the secret lies in the absolute unity of
> their religious principles, in the continuity of their language,
> and in the morality of their politics. Old indeed is the popular
> dictum "Unity Makes Power."
> What strength would a political organization have if the
> conscience of its people were riddled with heresies and fac-
> tions? None at all! It is a danger for all Brazilians, a danger
> threatening national unity, when anyone collaborates for the
> destruction of the religious unity of our fatherland. . . . In
> order to preserve the religious unity of our country, it is the duty
> of every Brazilian, even though he might hold no religious
> creed in his heart, to avoid any factions or heresies which might
> disturb the beneficial results of Catholicism in Brazil.
> It was this religion which prepared this land later to be our
> nation, which blessed us as free men, and which is making us a
> cultured people.[21]

Religious unity was thus equated with national unity, Roman

Catholicism with Brazilianism. One hears echoes of this idea in unexpected places, for example, in *The Masters and the Slaves*, where Gilberto Freyre asserts that "Catholicism was in reality the cement of our unity."[22]

One of the most articulate exponents of the conservative Roman Catholic brand of nationalism was Jackson de Figueiredo, a writer who believed in order, hierarchy, and the influence of the Catholic religion in politics. Figueiredo was also pro-Portuguese, recognizing and appreciating those values and institutions which Portugal had transmitted to Brazil. He closely identified nationalism with the Catholic tradition and emphasized the role the Roman Catholic Church had played in the formation of the Brazilian character. He particularly admired the Jesuits. The threats to Brazilian nationalism, he believed, came not from foreign powers but from Protestantism, Masonry, and Judaism.[23]

The two strongest forces opposing the development of Brazilian nationalism during this period were regionalism and internationalism. In as vast and varied a country as Brazil, regionalism had always been a threat to national unity. During the Regency period, it nearly destroyed the imperial structure. After the fall of the monarchy and throughout the Old Republic, it once again flourished. In 1926, a Brazilian Congress of Regionalism met in Recife—a traditional center of challenge to the national government. Although it was not "anti-national" in its philosophy or its pronouncements, the Congress was considerably less nationalistic than other organizations of the period.

At the opposite end of the spectrum were the internationalists, generally restricted to the upper class, who traveled widely, spoke several foreign languages, invested or deposited their money in New York, London, or Paris, and had a far more cosmopolitan range of interests than did the nationalists. They could upon occasion adopt nationalism for their own particular ends, and indeed some of them, Paulo Prado for example, were devoted nationalists. By and large, however, the upper class was international in orientation and for that reason increasingly scorned by the nationalists.

Both regionalism and internationalism were to prove far less dynamic forces than nationalism, which continued to gain momentum throughout the 1920's. Prosperity at home and peace abroad afforded the nationalists the opportunity to take a more honest look at their own country. Understanding more fully both their strengths and their weaknesses, the nationalists were eager to take the steps necessary to modernize their country. They advocated various reforms to effect such a modernization. That eagerness to remake the nation caused unrest and, on more than one occasion, rebellion. A coffee crisis in 1929, followed by a revolution in 1930, helped the nationalists to implement at least a part of their program.

5. Getúlio Vargas and Economic Nationalism

As long as coffee sold reasonably well on the world market and returned the profits necessary to maintain Brazil's progress, there was little that the nationalists could achieve in the way of basic political or economic reforms. Coffee sales fluctuated widely, but generally the profits kept returning. Under the Old Republic, Brazil enjoyed a virtual monopoly over the world market, furnishing 70 per cent of the coffee consumed. Coffee beans accounted for about 70 per cent of Brazil's exports during the decade of the 1920's. Clearly the well-being of the national economy depended on the sale of that single export. It is not surprising, therefore, that the three major coffee-producing states—São Paulo, Minas Gerais, and Rio de Janeiro—came to dominate all aspects of the national life. Well before the end of the empire, they exercised economic control over the country; after the advent of the republic, they assumed political direction as well. The first three civilian presidents, Prudente de Moraes Barros, Manuel Ferraz de Campos Salles, and Francisco de Paula Rodrigues Alves, were from São Paulo. With only a few exceptions, the other presidents also came from the three coffee states. National politics depended upon the desires of the governors of those states. As might be expected, the "coffee presidents" enacted policies highly favorable to the coffee interests. Commenting on the situation, in 1907, G. L. Lorillard, First Secretary at the U.S. legation, wrote to Secretary of State Elihu Root:

At the present time there exists a group of persons which is stronger than the Executive and Congress combined. As is universally admitted here, never before has the country and especially everyone connected with the Government been so much under the influence of the coffee planters as at the present and any measure which is seriously desired by that element is sure of immediate passage by Congress.[1]

The power of the coffee interests remained firm until the world economic crisis of the 1930's. Coffee prices plummeted from 22.5 cents a pound in 1929 to 8 cents in 1931. In the 1920's, Brazil shipped 805.8 million pounds of coffee abroad; in the 1930's, only 337 million pounds were sold. By 1930, São Paulo's warehouses groaned under the weight of 26 million bags of coffee beans—more than the world consumed in an entire year. The ensuing panic revealed the general sterility of the Old Republic. With the coffee money removed, its base of support was minimal.

The nationalists were among those disgruntled with the Old Republic. They suspected the coffee growers, who were intimately linked to the world markets, of being far too international in outlook. They also viewed with alarm the growing regionalism, which the permissive Constitution of 1891 seemed to encourage. The militia of the state of São Paulo, for example, had its own French military instructors and was at a strength and readiness capable of challenging the federal army. In some state capitals, the state flag flew from every mast, while one searched in vain for the Brazilian colors. The nationalists felt the time appropriate to establish a government better suited to the times and to their goals. They were therefore only too happy to cooperate with other forces desirous of change or jealous of the monopoly the coffee interests exercised over the nation's economic and political life.

The political forces outside the coffee triangle had long sought to wrest power from São Paulo, Minas Gerais, and Rio de Janeiro. Plucky Rio Grande do Sul provided the leadership for these forces, and in 1930, a split between the two major coffee states, São Paulo and Minas Gerais, over the presidential succession provided the opportunity for action. The dissident forces combined to form the Liberal Alliance. The elections of 1930 pitted the Alliance candidate, Getúlio Vargas of Rio Grande do Sul, against the government candidate, Júlio Prestes of São Paulo, a protégé of President Washington Luís. Defeated in the elections, which they complained were controlled by the government—a safe enough charge to make under the Old Republic—the adherents to the cause of the Liberal Alliance rebelled. Their forces marched on Rio de Janeiro from north, south, and west to prevent Prestes from taking office. Before a final showdown, the military intervened to depose President Luís and to summon Vargas to the presidency.

The Revolution of 1930 wrested power from the coffee interests and put it in the hands of an energetic *gaúcho*. Short, wiry, with a winning smile, and gifted with unusually keen political intuition, Getúlio Vargas understood and appreciated the potential of nationalism and the significance of the events of the 1920's. He characterized his own government as "profoundly nationalistic."[2] Upon taking office, he surrounded himself with idealistic *tenentes*, the young army officers who had supported the rebellion, and, in some cases, participated in the uprisings of 1922 and 1924. Vargas appointed these *tenentes* as state governors and as advisers. The army officers, as well as most of the nationalists, supported Vargas because he denounced the traditional politics of the Old Republic and offered hope for far-reaching reforms. He seemed to the nationalists a promising leader who would modernize Brazil, break with the outdated patterns of the past, and propel the country into the twentieth century. They preferred his authoritarian "renovation" (Vargas often employed the word *renovar* in discussing the future of the nation) to the masquerade of democracy that in their opinion had characterized the politics of the Old Republic.

The task confronting Vargas was neither easy nor unchallenged. He faced a variety of difficult problems: a civil war in 1932, in which São Paulo threatened the federal government and national unity; unemployment; falling export prices; declining hard currency reserves; and reviving militarism. Although most of the nation accorded him sympathetic support as he struggled with those problems, Brazilians never lost their desire to return to constitutional government. In 1933, Vargas unenthusiastically convoked a constituent assembly; the following year, it produced a new constitution and dutifully elected him to the presidency for a four-year term.

Still, Vargas did not lack for critics. The major challenges to his administration and policies came from the political parties. As in the past, the majority of the parties were regional groupings dependent on local personalities for their vigor. The only parties with strong national organizations were on the far left and the far right, the Communists and the Integralists.

The Communist Party (Partido Comunista Brasileiro, or PCB), founded in 1922, was particularly active during the early 1930's. One faction of the Party organized a popular front organization, the Aliança Nacional Libertadora (National Liberation Alliance, or ANL), which took shape in 1934. Luís Carlos Prestes, the romantic revolutionary who had led the march through the interior, now the leader of the PCB, served as honorary president. The ANL advocated the nationalization of foreign-owned businesses and attacked the latifundia system. The program attracted many supporters who did not consider themselves Communists but who passionately desired the modernization and development of Brazil. However, in 1935 the Party discredited itself by fomenting bloody uprisings in Recife, João Pessoa, and Rio de Janeiro, murdering officers and enlisted men. Vargas forced the Communists to disband, and they ceased to be an active force for a decade.

The right-wing Integralist party was founded in 1932, in frank imitation of the European fascist parties of the time. Like their European counterparts, the Integralists had their own symbol (the sigma), flag, and shirt color (green). Nationalistic and somewhat mystical in its appeal, the party emphasized order, hierarchy, and obedience. It advocated an "integral" state under a single authoritarian head of government. The party identified the "enemies of the nation" as democrats and Communists, as well as Masons and Jews. A cult of nationality was encouraged. Plínio Salgado and Gustavo Barroso, both of whom were writers of considerable talent, emerged as the party's principal intellectual leaders. Their speeches, essays, and books resounded with nationalistic phraseology. Salgado's *Nosso Brasil* (Our Brazil), published in 1937, is a glorification of the fatherland that recalls the exaggerations of Celso's work at the opening of the century. There was no official connection between the Integralist party, with its nationalist doctrine, and the government, with its nationalistic programs, although some highly placed officials, such as General Góes Monteiro, Chief of Staff of the Army, were Integralists. Nor was there any official link between the party and the Roman Catholic Church, although many members of the Catholic hierarchy lent the party their support and prestige.

The well-organized Communists and Integralists were a formidable threat to Vargas, and the weak, regional parties a hindrance to his plans for national unity. On November 10, 1937, claiming that the presidential campaign was threatening national tranquillity and harmony, Vargas cancelled the forthcoming elections, dismissed the Congress, closed the state legislatures and replaced the elected governors with his own appointees, and abolished all political parties. His actions established the authoritarian Estado Novo (New State), and he ruled unchallenged for the next eight years.

The major problems confronting Vargas during his long

first administration (1930–45) were economic ones. The sudden fall of coffee prices on the world market had ruined Brazil financially. There were two possible long-range solutions to this crisis. The first was to diversify the economy. Brazil had traditionally been dependent on a single raw product for export: if it was not brazilwood, it was sugar; if not sugar, gold; if not gold, coffee. Dependent on the whims of foreign markets, Brazil had little control over its own economic destiny. Diversification would obviously eliminate some of the risks that reliance on a single export entailed. A second solution, and a corollary of the first, was to accelerate industrialization. On the one hand, industrialization would help to diversify the economy; on the other, it would help to prevent precious foreign exchange from being spent to import what could be manufactured at home. Vargas adopted both solutions and launched an energetic economic development program. In introducing government planning and participation on a large scale into the economic life of the country, Vargas fulfilled the aspirations of the nationalists, who were becoming more economically oriented.

The Vargas era marked a definite shift of emphasis from cultural and political nationalism to economic nationalism. Economic nationalism was by no means a novelty of the 1930's, although it was in that decade that it received primary emphasis for the first time. As we have seen in the preceding chapters, the roots of economic nationalism extended back into the eighteenth century. Its manifestations were sporadic but intense in the nineteenth century. The British and the Portuguese particularly felt its barbs. A fiery article that appeared in a Rio de Janeiro newspaper, *A Liga Americana,* in 1839 exemplified the form that incipient economic nationalism took. Headlined "Measures Appropriate for Developing Brazilian Nationality and Industry," the article decried the lack of protection for local industry and criticized the foreign merchants resident in Brazil.[3]

Modern economic nationalism in Brazil has its origins in the writings of Alberto Tôrres (1865–1917). In a series of books published between 1909 and 1915, Tôrres equated economic development and nationalism. The equation was simple but important. The nationalists would later seize upon it as the magic formula for the future. Tôrres was clearly disillusioned with the Old Republic. He argued that the federal government should be granted greater powers. Even then, however, it could not be expected to exercise "real sovereignty" or manifest "true nationalism" if the nation did not control its own sources of wealth, its industry, and its commerce. He discussed this point in detail in his *O Problema Nacional Brasileiro* (The National Brazilian Problem), published in 1914:

> Above all else, the independence of a people is founded on their economy and their finances. . . . In order for a nation to remain independent it is imperative to preserve the vital organs of nationality: the principal sources of wealth, the industries of primary products, the instrumentalities and agents of economic circulation, transportation and internal commerce. There must be no monopolies and no privileges. . . . A people cannot be free if they do not control their own sources of wealth, produce their own food, and direct their own industry and commerce.[4]

This pioneer economic nationalist argued that the Old Republic had turned over its economic destiny to foreigners, who had sown their capital without restriction and were reaping an abundant harvest. He proposed a limit on foreign investments. Without a stronger government and without control over its own economic destiny, Brazil would continue to be "a dispersed, amorphous nation in an almost liquid state . . . a nation composed of admirable individuals morally united but with no social character, an assembly of races and types without a national model"—in short, "a nation without nationality."[5] Tôrres clearly indicated the path economic nationalism should take. The nationalists began to follow his guideposts in the 1930's. Certainly Tôrres' ideas fitted the plans of Getúlio Vargas perfectly; a second edition of *O Problema Nacional Brasileiro* was published in 1933, just as the nationalists' campaign for economic development got underway.

The nationalists insisted that only through economic development could Brazil become truly independent. The nation's traditional economic dependence had inhibited its exercise of political independence. The nationalists realized that Brazil in fact still retained its colonial status, that colonial economic institutions and patterns survived. A rural oligarchy, in alliance with foreign capital, perpetuated the mercantilist system, and the vestiges of colonialism arrested the nation's development.[6] Beginning in the 1930's, therefore, Brazilian nationalism, like that flourishing in the rest of Latin America and in other underdeveloped areas, became increasingly characterized by resentment of foreign capital and foreign personnel, suspicion of private enterprise, a growing preference for state ownership, emphasis on industrialization, encouragement of domestic production, and a desire to create or nationalize certain key industries such as oil, steel, power, and transportation.

The struggle to industrialize Brazil reached back to the beginning of the nineteenth century. Although King João VI had lifted the ban on manufacturing in Brazil as early as 1808, the real impetus for industrialization came later—in 1844, when the British trade preference was ended and the first significant tariff enacted, and in 1850, when termination of the slave trade freed capital for investment. In 1850, there were only fifty factories in Brazil; forty years later, there were more than six hundred factories, employing some 54,000 workers. The textile industry was the most highly developed; other important industries were food, chemical, wood, and metal products. In 1882, the Associação Industrial, an organization to encourage and protect national industry, was formed. The association's publication, *O Industrial,* urged industrialization as the means to obtain economic independence and resolve major national problems. Nationalists at the turn of the century also voiced their opposition to the increasing number of foreign companies. Between 1899 and 1910, only 41 national companies were formed, but 160 foreign companies were authorized to operate in Brazil.

The leaders of the Old Republic had made repeated attempts to industrialize the country. Their efforts met with dramatic success after the outbreak of World War I, when isolation from Europe forced the nation to rely on its own industry. It was during this period that São Paulo emerged as the dynamic center of the new industrialization. The total value of the products manufactured in that state tripled between 1915 and 1920. The progress was so impressive that in 1928, President Washington Luís observed that industrialization had become a way of life in Brazil; at the same time, Cassiano Ricardo saluted this urban, industrial future in his celebrated poem *Martim Cererê.*

The world economic depression of the 1930's further stimulated industrialization, as Brazil was once again forced either to manufacture its own goods or to do without. New textile, leather-processing, chemical, and machine industries appeared. By 1938, industrial production was valued at over a billion dollars, twice that of agricultural production. World War II provided a third impulse to economic growth. During the war years, Brazil built up vast foreign-exchange reserves from its sale of goods abroad. These were all squandered within two years after the end of the war. The new foreign-exchange crisis again forced the country to substitute locally produced goods for imported ones. During those industrial booms, São Paulo retained its economic leadership. Names such as Matarazzo, the captain of a vast industrial empire centered in São Paulo, symbolized the growth of big business.

By mid-century, Brazil had become the most industrialized nation in Latin America. Industrialization set in motion changes that revolutionized Brazilian life. It created new centers of wealth and of political power. It challenged the traditional social structure by giving preference to personal skills and adaptability over family lineage. Under the impact of industrialization, the middle class grew rapidly in both size and influence. The newly organized trade unions welcomed reform and on occasion exerted pressure for it. The Vargas years marked the turning point in all these developments.

Yet, industrial growth depended on the well-being of the vast agricultural sector of the economy. Vargas recognized the importance of the coffee industry, which continued to account for approximately 50 per cent of the nation's exports. He encouraged the signing of international agreements under which nations agreed to purchase specified amounts of coffee; these agreements replaced the discredited valorization scheme, under which surpluses were stored at government expense until prices rose. The President also encouraged the development of the cattle industry, and the mechanization of the sugar industry.

Industrialization also depended on the protection of the country's natural resources. The nationalists had long been critical of foreign exploitation of Brazil's natural wealth. In the 1920's, they had mounted a campaign against Percival Farquhar, an adventurous North American investor in Brazilian railroads and mines. Farquhar ran into fierce opposition from the nationalists when he obtained the Itabira iron-ore concession. President Arthur Bernardes took up the nationalist cause and eventually forced cancellation of the concession. The final result was an amendment to the Constitution of 1891: "Mines and mineral deposits necessary for national security and the land in which they are found cannot be transferred to foreigners." (Article 72.) The amendment was a major victory for the nationalists. A similar restriction appeared in the Constitution of 1934: "The law will regulate the progressive nationalization of mines, mineral deposits, and waterfalls or other sources of energy, as well as of the industries considered as basic or essential to the economic and military defense of the country." (Article 119.) The Constitution of 1937 included the same provision except that the word "nation" was substituted for "country." (Article 144.) Accordingly, Vargas placed restrictions on foreign companies that discouraged or controlled their exploitation of Brazil's natural resources. In 1942, he established the corporation Companhia Vale do Rio Doce (Doce River Valley Company) to exploit the rich iron-ore deposits of Itabira; iron ore production quintupled between 1939 and 1951, with most of the increase occurring after 1946.

Vargas further boosted national pride and self-sufficiency by authorizing the construction of the first steel mill in Brazil. Plans for the mill were drawn up in 1940, and in 1946 the mill at Volta Redonda went into operation. By 1955, it was producing 646,000 tons of steel; by 1963, this output was doubled.

But the symbol of economic nationalism, for Brazilians as well as for all Latin Americans, was petroleum. The nationalists believed that the discovery and exploitation of oil was not only economically desirable but would guarantee Brazil's achievement of world-power status. At first, Vargas understood the importance of petroleum purely as an economic matter. He established the National Petroleum Council to coordinate and intensify the search for oil, and in 1939, the first successful well was drilled: oil gushed forth from the Brazilian soil. The nationalists—who were unwilling to see the oil, or the profits from its exploitation, siphoned off to foreign countries—then called for the creation of a national oil industry. Oil soon came to dominate their thoughts, and in the words of one contemporary nationalist, it became "the backbone of nationalism."[7] In time, Vargas came to see the emotional significance of oil to the nationalists, and he duly paid homage to the symbol. "Whoever hands over petroleum to foreigners threatens our own independence," he remarked.[8]

During his second administration (1951–54), Vargas exploited that symbol in a bid for wider support. In 1951, he proposed the creation of Petrobrás, a state monopoly of all activities connected with the exploration for and development of petroleum resources. Its creation, in 1953, followed a national campaign in which the cry *"O petróleo é nosso!"* ("The Oil Is Ours!") echoed throughout the land. The establishment of Petrobrás was a victory for the nationalists. They had triumphed over those who argued that it would be more economical for experienced foreign companies to drill for oil and pay Brazil a royalty on whatever was pumped out. The nationalists would have none of that argument. At any rate, the question was an emotional, not an economic, one. In the words of one nationalist, "the Brazilian people . . . struggled for the creation of the state oil monopoly because they believed that in that struggle they were defending national sovereignty."[9] The confessed goal of Petrobrás was to contribute to the economic independence of Brazil: Vargas' own phrase was "to create national liberty."[10] The nationalists succeeded in convincing the masses that a national oil industry represented sovereignty, independence, power, and well-being. For the first time, they stirred up popular support for a nationalist cause. Petrobrás remains the major single permanent achievement of the nationalists. The emotions aroused by its creation recall the dramatic nationalization of the oil industry in Mexico, in 1938.

The growth of industry and the attendant urbanization provided the conditions that allowed Vargas to make other contributions to Brazilian nationalism. One of the most significant of these was his alteration of the source of leadership of the nationalist movement by greatly strengthening the federal government. Vargas helped to create the strongest federal government to that time in Brazil; it took over much of the power and influence formerly enjoyed by the state governments. Within the federal government itself, the executive emerged supreme. A stronger, more vigorous president helped to bring a new order and unity to the nation. The expanding road, rail, and air networks facilitated Vargas' ability to reach out to the remotest regions of Brazil with a speed his predecessors never dreamed possible.

Vargas also used the public school system to encourage the growth of national feelings. In 1930, he created the first Ministry of Education, and installed his trusted adviser Francisco Campos as its first Minister. Among Campos' policies to nationalize education, perhaps the most important was the requirement that all instruction be given in the Portuguese language; the regulation was aimed at accelerating the Brazilianization of European immigrants, particularly in the South, where there were large concentrations of Germans, Poles, and Italians. In a speech in Blumenau, Santa Catarina, a center of European settlement, the Vargas-appointed governor, Nerêu Ramos, defended the new education policy:

> It cannot surprise anyone that the Estado Novo is taking the necessary steps to integrate within the Brazilian soul once and for all those born on our soil who are alienated from it by language, customs, traditions, and education. . . .
> The hour of rebirth is upon us. With the Constitution of November 10, a stronger and more united Brazil emerges. The first condition for that supreme national realization is that in none of its regions prevails or predominates, by neglect of the government or by resistance from aliens, a language which is not ours, traditions other than those from our own past, glories that are not connected with our heroes.[11]

Stronger emphasis was also placed on the teaching of Brazilian history; for the first time, chairs of Brazilian history were established in the universities. The aims of the Vargas educational program were summed up in 1940 by Minister of War (and later President) General Eurico Dutra. "The principal objective of education is to create a national consciousness," he said, and he went on to emphasize that the schools had the duty to encourage "a mentality capable of disposing public opinion favorably toward nationalism."[12] Vargas also created the National Service of Historic and Artistic Patrimony, one of whose principal projects was the creation of the Imperial Museum in Petropolis, a monument to the glories of the empire.

Vargas did not hesitate to use the institutions and power of the state to promote nationalist goals—a method that was very much in vogue in Europe in the 1930's and which was being perfected by the Latin American *caudillos*. As a result, the state replaced the intellectual as the primary guardian and promoter of nationalism.[13] Although many intellectuals were employed by the government in the 1930's and throughout most of the 1940's, they played a secondary role. With the end of the Estado Novo, they regained their position of leadership. Yet the intellectuals would never again exercise the monopoly over the nationalist movement that they had held prior to 1930—too many others vied for this position.

Vargas can also be credited with broadening the base of support of nationalist policies to include increasing numbers of the military, industrialists, intellectuals, politicians, and middle class. Most important, he succeeded in winning the urban proletariat to the nationalist cause. He achieved this partly by reaching out to them through the school system, the growing number of newspapers, and the burgeoning radio industry. He also won their support through his governmental policies. Vargas nationalized the job market by limiting the number of foreigners who could be employed and by restricting many public offices to native-born Brazilians. He also restricted immigration, a policy sanctioned by

the Constitutions of 1934 and 1937. Through his paternal
labor and welfare programs—the establishment of minimum
wages and maximum hours, job security, paid vacations,
among others—he made the workers feel that they had more
at stake in the government than ever before. The nationalism
Vargas expressed came to have a practical meaning for the
working class. It meant more than slogans; it meant jobs,
personal pride, economic advancement. In a very practical
way they could identify with it.

But Vargas also excited the imagination of the masses with
less tangible aspects of nationalism. For example, he adopted
the theme, popularized by the nationalists in the 1920's, that
the Brazilian West was a key to the realization of the national potential. Vargas often defined his plans for a march
to the hinterlands, the "March to the West." The development of that great, promised land was to be "the true sense
of Brazilianism."[14] In his essay *A Marcha para o Oeste, Couto
de Magalhães e Getúlio Vargas* (The March to the West,
Couto de Magalhães and Getúlio Vargas), Ildefonso Escobar
hailed Vargas as the heir of the *bandeirantes* and the realizer
of the dreams of countless patriots who had struggled to
open up the Brazilian interior. Although the essay exaggerated Vargas' accomplishments, his administration did in reality enact programs for the arid *sertão* of the Northeast and
the slumbering Amazon Valley.

The economic policies of the Vargas government also appealed to the growing number of industrialists, who had
emerged as an important factor in the economy. They were
not concerned with exporting raw materials or importing
manufactured goods. They produced for the internal market,
which they wanted to protect and to expand. They appreciated the benefits of economic nationalism. The more enlightened industrialists also understood that Vargas' labor
policies would in the long run increase the market for their
goods.

Despite Vargas' many contributions to national growth, the country began to chafe under his authoritarian rule after a decade and a half. The Brazilians sardonically noted that they supported the Allied effort to eliminate dictatorship in Europe while living under their own dictator at home. By late 1944, their desire to return to a democratic system was unmistakably clear. Vargas, acceding to the mounting pressure, agreed to hold elections in December, 1945. The government relaxed its political controls, and a variety of political parties emerged. Three of them achieved national importance and, despite their weaknesses, can be regarded as the first nationwide democratic parties in Brazilian history. The Partido Social Democrático (Social Democratic Party, or PSD), founded by Vargas himself, represented urban, moderate, middle-class interests. The União Democrática Nacional (National Democratic Union, or UDN), founded by the opposition to Vargas, tended to support conservative doctrines and to favor the interests of the traditional oligarchy. The Partido Trabalhista Brasileiro (Brazilian Labor Party, or PTB), also founded by Vargas, appealed to the workers and expressed a leftist ideology. The leadership of the PTB was predominately middle-class in origin and was vociferously nationalistic. The three parties were to contribute significantly to the growth of Brazilian democracy.

As the date for the elections approached, Vargas hinted that he might like to continue in office. Rumors spread that the President was once again going to cancel an election. In late October, 1945, the military intervened to depose the President and guarantee the elections. The candidate of the PSD and PTB, General Eurico Dutra, was elected and took office in 1946 for a five-year term. Dutra proved to be not unsympathetic to Vargas, who at the last moment had given the General his endorsement, and his administration continued many of the Vargas policies. Dutra's proposed five-year development plan also pleased the nationalists, who saw their hopes for an industrialized Brazil beginning to be realized.

In the elections of 1950, Vargas was returned to office as democratically elected president. If anything, he was more nationalistic in both his pronouncements and his actions during his second administration than in his first. As we have seen, it was during this administration that he created Petrobrás and attempted to extend government control over energy and power resources; he also inaugurated his own five-year plan for industrialization.

Ironically, much of Brazil's remarkable industrial progress during these years was due to the mounting investment of foreign capitalists, whom the nationalists, as always, suspected of a variety of evil motives. Vargas became even more outspoken in his criticism of foreign ownership of industry, and he launched a bitter attack against foreign investors, accusing them of "bleeding Brazil." The nationalists cheered each pronouncement. Yet funds continued to flow in from abroad, and industrialization expanded at a rapid pace.

Clearly, Vargas had mastered the rhetoric of the nationalists and adapted it to his own purposes. He relied upon the popular appeal of nationalism more than he had in the past, and these nationalist feelings strengthened his second administration which was less stably anchored than his first.

Yet after two years in office, the aging President found himself in grave difficulties. The increasingly complex social and economic problems facing Brazil puzzled him. He had also lost some of his flexibility and adroitness. Showing an inability to govern within the framework of the democratic system, he resorted to some of his former strong-arm tactics. Corruption surrounded the presidency, although Vargas himself was apparently an honest man. When the attempted assassination of a persistent critic was traced to Vargas' personal bodyguard, the army stepped in once again and demanded his resignation. Vargas replied by committing suicide, on August 25, 1954. He left behind a suicide note (over which there has been speculation as to its authenticity), which echoed his nationalist sentiments. He wrote of "years of domination and looting by international economic and financial groups" and of "a subterranean campaign of international groups joined with the national groups revolting against the regime of workers' guarantees," and boasted: "I fought against the looting of Brazil."[15] The note has become a nationalistic document, and nationalists have not hesitated to use it in attacking their enemies both at home and abroad.

An era ended with the death of Getúlio Vargas. For nearly a generation, he had guided, directly or indirectly, the course of Brazilian development. During those years Brazilian nationalism began to follow a more economically oriented course, its leadership passed from the hands of the intellectuals to the government, and its base of support expanded. In the meantime, an entirely new school of nationalists, imbued with the ideology of economic development and accustomed to the government's role in fostering and directing nationalism, had emerged. Greater activists than their nineteenth- and early twentieth-century predecessors, they were eager to assume political leadership and to implement their ideas. The opportunity was offered to them in the following decade.

6. Action and Reaction

Under the administrations of Presidents Juscelino Kubit-schek (1956–61), Jânio Quadros (January 31, 1961–August 25, 1961), and João Goulart (September 7, 1961–March 31, 1964), the nationalist movement gained supporters and strength, nationalist doctrines received greater attention from official policy-makers, and nationalists played a more active role in government. Those eight years marked the high point in the success and influence of the nationalists. Their heyday abruptly ended on April 1, 1964, when the military—suspicious of the path down which the nationalists were guiding Brazil—seized control of the government in a *coup d'état*.

During the dynamic Kubitschek-Quadros-Goulart era, Bra-zilian nationalism manifested four major characteristics. First, the political left took over the leadership of the move-ment. The Integralist party was the last major party of the right to appeal to nationalistic feelings. After its suppression, in 1937, the nationalist cause was adopted by the parties of the left. Contemporary nationalists have relied heavily on the Marxist lexicon—a fact that has exposed the movement to the criticism that it is guided or dominated by the Com-munists. Such an accusation is not only false, it also oversim-plifies the complexity of Brazilian nationalism and obscures efforts to understand it.

Second, nationalist leaders became increasingly critical of foreign economic domination. We have already looked at the early critics of foreign enterprise, beginning with Azeredo

Coutinho and continuing through Alberto Tôrres. Contemporary criticism has been even harsher, as in this not untypical comment: "Neocolonialism, that is, economic colonialism, subordinates the economy of the underdeveloped country to the economy of the superdeveloped country. It takes hold of all the important sources of income. The population of the dominated country is kept ignorant, poor, feeble, incapable of any reaction. It inculcates in the poorer nation an inferiority complex."[1]

Third, the nationalists directed their strongest attack against the United States. They had an obvious target. The United States was the largest single investor in Brazil. Its investments rose from $28 million in 1914, to $577 million in 1950, to $1.5 billion in 1960 (about half of the total foreign investment in Brazil). Any campaign against foreign capital would automatically assume predominantly anti-Yankee tones. Then, too, the U.S. government had become identified with the oligarchy and with the preservation of the status quo in Brazil. The United States was viewed as a static force, hostile to the renovating aspirations of the nationalists. It appeared as an enemy whose influence and presence had to be challenged and defeated if nationalism was to triumph. The former anti-Portuguese, anti-British, and anti-Spanish American attitudes all but disappeared. Uncle Sam served as the mid-twentieth-century whipping boy. In 1893, Eduardo Prado had applied the first lash in his *A Ilusão Americana* (The American Illusion), a book reissued in 1961. Prado had violently attacked the United States and "the absorbent, imperialist, and tyrannical policies of North American diplomacy." He concluded bitterly: "There is no Latin American nation that has not suffered in its relations with the United States."[2] The tone, the phrasing, the themes became part of the nationalist baggage, and since World War II, Brazilian politicians have cultivated anti-Americanism as a convenient and certain means to arouse national feeling.

Finally, the nationalists paid even greater attention to the question of economic development. Defining nationalism as "the political consciousness of development,"[3] they saw it as the sole force capable of modernizing the nation. The doctrine of "developmental nationalism" that took shape in the 1950's called for government control of natural resources, limitations on foreign capital, continuing industrialization, and increased trade with all nations. "Developmental nationalism" was considered to be the only way to liberate Brazil, to unchain it from the past and propel it into the future. The concept attracted many who did not necessarily support all of the hard-core nationalist causes.

These four characteristics of Brazilian nationalism were clearly evident during the administration of President Juscelino Kubitschek. Kubitschek placed particular emphasis on economic development, which he regarded as the key to national independence: "The nationalism which we espouse is one which is based upon our development. The nationalism propitious for Brazil would tend to place it on the level of the rest of the countries of the world so that it could speak as an equal without subservience, without fear, without any feeling of inferiority."[4] Kubitschek promised his countrymen "fifty years' progress in five," and to a large extent he fulfilled that promise. Brazil's rate of economic growth during his administration was 7 per cent a year; during the 1950's as a whole, it was nearly three times that of the rest of Latin America.

Industry boomed under Kubitschek's leadership. To supply the desperately needed power for industrialization, the President authorized the construction of the gigantic Furnas hydroelectric project and the impressive Três Marias Dam on the São Francisco river. The principal heavy industry, steel, continued to expand. An automobile industry was also created. By May, 1967, a million and a half cars had rolled off the assembly lines of the ten automobile producers. Tractors and trucks also went into production. Brazil soon not only manufactured enough automobiles to meet its own needs, but began to export cars, tractors, and trucks to its neighbors. Kubitschek also focused attention on the perennial plight of the arid Northeast by creating the Superintendência do Desenvolvimento do Nordeste (Superintendency of the Development of the Northeast, or SUDENE), in 1959.

Kubitschek will probably be best remembered for realizing one of the nationalists' oldest dreams: he moved the capital from the coast to the interior. In 1956, he created the Companhia Urbanizadora da Nova Capital (Urbanization Company of the New Capital) to take charge of building the new city of Brasília. Lúcio Costa prepared a daring plan for the new capital, which Oscar Niemeyer matched with imaginative designs for the federal buildings. Work on Brasília began in 1957 and continued at a frantic pace. On April 21, 1960, Kubitschek inaugurated the new capital, an expensive but magnificent gesture that Brazil was at last going to develop its untapped hinterland, so long a "promised land." An ambitious program of "highways of national union" was undertaken to connect the new capital with the rest of the nation. Roads were built from Brasília to Belém, 1,400 miles to the north; to Fortaleza, 1,060 miles to the northeast; to Belo Horizonte, 400 miles to the southeast, and thence to Rio de Janeiro, São Paulo, and the south.

Kubitschek's programs to develop Brazil were as expensive as they were grandiose. To meet the costs, the government simply turned on the printing presses and let the currency flow out. In 1955, there were 69 billion cruzeiros in circulation; in 1961, 202 billion. Inflation, which had plagued the country since the end of World War II, continued to mount. The International Monetary Fund expressed dismay over the situation and threatened to withhold loans until the government adopted more orthodox financial methods. The nationalists, however, regarded inflation as a spur to industrialization; they also resented outside interference, no matter how well intentioned. Kubitschek himself felt that the stabilization policies urged by the IMF would slow down his development plans. To the delight of the nationalists, he denounced the Fund for trying to delay the industrialization of Brazil, and in June, 1959, he broke off negotiations with the international organization.

The free-spending Kubitschek administration was succeeded by the short-lived government of Jânio Quadros. Quadros' impressive record as reform governor of the state of São Paulo had raised hopes that he would be able to extend his reforms to the national level. (His campaign symbol, the broom, revealed the emphasis he gave to "cleaning up" the government.) Although Quadros was the candidate of the conservative National Democratic Union, he ran on his own personal platform, and won an overwhelming victory, piling up 5.6 million votes, nearly equal to the combined total received by the two other principal candidates. Yet beyond the pledge to clean up the government, Quadros' policies seemed vague and even contradictory. A maverick in politics, Quadros did not share the UDN's suspicions of the nationalists. On the contrary, he sympathized with some aspects of the nationalist program—such as restrictions on foreign capital—and clearly appreciated its growing popular appeal. But on the whole, the new President appeared to view internal affairs rather conventionally. In foreign affairs, on the other hand, Quadros displayed a flair for the experimental. His greatest contribution to Brazilian nationalism was the introduction of an independent foreign policy.

Brazilian public opinion had long demanded that the country play a role in world affairs. Brazil had contributed 25,000 troops to the Allied campaign in Italy during World War II —it was the only Latin American country to participate in the European war—and had sent men to the United Nations forces in the Middle East and in the Congo. That Brazilians aspire to play an even greater role in international affairs is indicated by the titles of such books as Manoel Meira de Vasconcellos' *Brasil, Potência Militar* (Brazil, A Military Power) and Pimentel Gomes' *O Brasil entre as Cinco Maiores Potências ao Fim dêste Século* (Brazil Among the Five Major Powers by the End of the Century). It is not uncommon to read in the contemporary popular press such optimistic statements as, "within this generation we will see Brazil transformed into a world power."[5] Such ideas excite and flatter a large portion of the population.

Under the prodding of the nationalists, the Brazilians reassessed their own international interests and strengths. Brazil became more aware of its advantageous geopolitical position. The giant of South America, it comprises half of the continent's territory and population and borders on all but two of the nations of that continent. With an extensive coastline, it dominates the South Atlantic and is strategically located vis-à-vis Africa. Its racial amalgamation gives it a unique position in the world community.

The foreign policy of Quadros pursued two basic goals: to encourage the economic and political development of Brazil and to display greater diplomatic independence. To achieve these goals, Quadros set out to disengage Brazil from the Cold War. Since the end of World War II, Brazil had been firmly attached to the Western bloc. The nationalists believed that rigid adherence to that bloc, with the consequent subservience to the United States, inhibited Brazil's scope of action. In particular, they were eager to seek out new non-Western markets for Brazilian goods. The nationalists envisioned eager consumers not only for Brazil's agricultural products—coffee, sugar, cocoa, and tobacco—but also for the increasing array of its industrial products. One of the potential new markets was Communist China, and in August, 1961, President Quadros dispatched a mission to that country to explore the possibilities for a trade agreement. (It was from this mission that Vice President Goulart was summoned to assume the presidency following Quadros' resignation.)

The disengagement from the Cold War not only brought Brazil closer to the East but, of at least equal significance, put it into closer contact with those countries of Asia and Africa that believed national development should take precedence over international alliances. Not only did Brazil share much in common with those countries, which suffer from similar social and economic problems, but it saw a unique opportunity for leadership among those nations that it could not hope to enjoy in the traditional alliance with the West.

Quadros particularly sought to exert leadership among the newly emergent African states. Both geography and history provided a convincing rationale for his hopes. Brazil is the closest country in the Western hemisphere to Africa. During the three centuries in which the slave trade flourished, Africa furnished a high percentage of Brazil's population, and the African presence is still very much a part of contemporary Brazil. Quadros believed that his country could serve as a link between the newly independent African nations and the West. Accordingly, he recognized the new African states, exchanged ambassadors with them, dispatched trade missions, offered fellowships to African students, and established an Afro-Asian Institute. He also denounced Portuguese colonial policies, which Brazilian politicians had previously either accepted or declined to comment on. The program was broad and audacious. The Negro community in Brazil welcomed and approved the new attitude toward the African states. An African viewpoint was expressed by Joseph Medupe Johnson, Minister of Labor of Nigeria, who said that Brazil became known in his country only after the election of Quadros.[6]

Brazil made its independence felt in the Western hemisphere through its treatment of Cuba. As a presidential candidate, Quadros had made a leisurely visit to the island, at a time when the United States was putting pressure on the

Latin American governments to break relations with the government of Fidel Castro. Later, as president, he welcomed to Brasília Ernesto Che Guevara, whom he decorated with the highest national honor, the Order of the Southern Cross. The apparent objective of the Brazilian government was to put itself in a position to play the role of mediator between Havana and Washington. In the past, Brazil had often acted as the intermediary between Spanish-speaking South America and the United States—a role Rio-Branco had perfected. Quadros sought to expand that role, but he gave himself little time in which to do so. In August, 1961, after less than seven months in office, he suddenly resigned. His departure from Brasília stunned the nation, and his abrupt decision still begs explanation. Quadros' cryptic letter of resignation did little to dispel the mystery. Strangely echoing Vargas' suicide note, Quadros spoke of those "forces"—"foreign" and "terrible"—that opposed and hindered him. "I wanted Brazil for the Brazilians," he wrote.

The resignation shifted the spotlight to Vice President João Goulart, who had been exchanging toasts with Mao Tse-tung in Peking. Goulart could not be described as a popular figure; he had been re-elected to the vice presidency with a scant one-third of the vote. The military, long suspicious of his labor policies and unsympathetic to his general political orientation, moved to block his accession to office as prescribed by the constitution. Public opinion rallied to Goulart's support to demand that the constitution be observed. The officers agreed to a compromise: Goulart could take the oath of office as president but he would share his powers with a prime minister under a new parliamentary arrangement. On September 7, 1961, Goulart officially put on the sash of office.

In his foreign policy, the new President took his cue from his predecessor. Like Quadros, he courted Cuba. He dispatched a trusted military aide to Havana in an attempt to bring about an understanding between the Castro government and Washington. He welcomed a Chinese trade mission to Rio de Janeiro, and re-established diplomatic relations with Moscow (they had been suspended since 1947) and with other Communist governments. Diplomatic missions were also dispatched to such diverse countries as Algeria and Ceylon. The desire for trade and prestige were two reasons for the recognition of Communist governments and the establishment of diplomatic posts in neutralist nations; the compelling psychological motive was the desire to exert independence of action.

San Tiago Dantas, at one time Foreign Minister under Goulart, often used the expression "independent foreign policy," in his speeches and writings. In 1962, he wrote that "the Brazilian people realized, and all countries understood, that Brazil had taken an international position, and that position was neither arbitrary nor provisional but corresponded to the permanent interests and aspirations of our nationality." In an official report published the same year he emphasized that the position was above all an independent one: "We can say that the international position of our country . . . has constantly evolved toward an attitude of independence in relation to the political-military blocs."[7]

There was much that was old in the Quadros-Goulart foreign policy. It supported the traditional policies of peaceful solution of international disputes, nonintervention, self-determination, and international order. What was strikingly new was the determination to exercise independent leadership and to gain recognition on a much broader scale than ever before. Rio-Branco had weakened Brazil's ties with Europe in favor of a closer friendship with the United States; the nationalists of the mid-twentieth century were prepared to de-emphasize those connections in favor of a new alliance between the underdeveloped nations of Latin America, Africa, and Asia.

In domestic affairs, Goulart proved to be an erratic, opportunistic, but effective ally for the nationalists. He said the right things; he condemned foreign economic imperialism; he made vague promises to carry out reforms. Thus, a large percentage of the nationalists supported him.

Soon after Goulart took office, his administration enacted two measures long sought by the nationalists. The first of these was the creation of Eletrobrás, a national agency to coordinate a system of state and private electric power plants. Eletrobrás gave the Brazilian government control over a power resource vital to the future development of the country.

The second measure limited the profits that foreign companies could withdraw from Brazil. A considerable percentage of all industry in Brazil was still foreign owned or controlled. Foreigners contributed more than 70 per cent of the capital invested in the thirty-four largest private companies, and more than 30 per cent invested in the 650 corporations with capital of one million dollars or more. They owned outright 28 per cent of the leading 1,820 Brazilian corporations, an increase of 3 per cent in the past ten years. Private citizens and companies of the United States accounted for 37 per cent of the foreign investments, making the United States by far the largest single investor in Brazil; of the thirty largest companies in Brazil, six were U.S. firms. The nationalists charged that foreign investors received higher profits from their Brazilian investments than they did from investments in the United States or Europe; they claimed that over the years foreigners had taken out of Brazil many times the sum of their original investments, and they painted a dreary picture of a Brazil being bled white by greedy Wall Street types.

One of the most vocal of the critics was Leonel Brizzola, brother-in-law of Goulart, who in the early 1960's emerged as the most demagogic of the radical nationalist politicians. Brizzola expressed the fear that Brazil was going to be absorbed by the United States; he called for the expulsion not only of American businessmen but also of the Peace Corps. When he was governor of the state of Rio Grande do Sul, his state expropriated the National Telephone Company, a subsidiary of the International Telephone and Telegraph Company of New York, to which he paid $400,000 for assets valued at $8 million. The U.S. government immediately protested, but Brazilians in general approved the bold action. When other states discussed taking similar action, the federal government undertook to negotiate a settlement with the management of the foreign-owned utilities. In 1963, the government signed a "memorandum of understanding" with the American and Foreign Power Company, and in October, 1964, it purchased the ten Brazilian subsidiaries of the company for $135 million—a vastly inflated sum, in the opinion of the nationalists.

The nationalist case on foreign investment—although overstated—had great popular appeal. It provided a simple and understandable explanation for low wages, high prices, and poverty, all of which could be blamed on foreign exploitation. The Goulart administration relied heavily on the foreign-profits issue to gain popular support. On September 3, 1962, Goulart signed the law limiting profit remittances. According to the provisions of the law, all foreign capital was to be registered with the Brazilian government and, in effect, no profit remittances in excess of 10 per cent of invested capital were permitted. The most immediate result of the law was a drastic drop in foreign investments: from a $120 million-a-year average in the period 1956–61 to only $18 million in 1962. In an economy as fragile as Brazil's, the drop in investments forewarned of future difficulties. However, for the moment, the cries of the Cassandras could not be heard over the huzzas of the nationalists.

The promulgation of the profits remittance law and the

creation of Eletrobrás seemed to give further indication that nationalism was in the ascendancy in Brazil. How could it be otherwise when one president after another enacted policies from the nationalist program and spoke in an increasingly pronounced nationalist rhetoric? By so doing they lent prestige and power to the movement. On certain key issues, they even provided overt leadership for the heterogeneous nationalists.

It was, indeed, an amazingly diverse group that held the banner of nationalism aloft. Their concurrence on the need for reform, modernization, industrialization, and national economic and diplomatic independence, and their suspicion of foreign exploitation, gave them a superficial unity under which swirled a myriad of conflicting plans and ideas for the achievement of their goals. In very general terms, moving from left to center on the spectrum of nationalist supporters, one encountered the intellectuals and students, the urban proletariat and the middle class, and certain elements among the military and industrialists. The politicians took up various positions along the spectrum.

The intellectuals made the most original contribution to the nationalist movement, supplying much of the material for the nationalist argument—a role they have historically played. During the 1950's and early 1960's, they contributed an outpouring of books and articles, many of them serious studies, others merely tiresome diatribes. Among the more successful works were those of Barbosa Lima Sobrinho, a former governor of Pernambuco and federal congressman, and a historian and writer of merit, who spoke out against the foreign power companies; Cândido Mendes de Almeida, the distinguished educator and economist, who wrote about the link between nationalism and development; and José Honório Rodrigues, one of Brazil's outstanding historians, whose fine work supporting Quadros' independent foreign policy was published in English under the title *Brazil and Africa*.

The intellectuals concentrated their attention, however, on the problem of economic development. Beginning in the second Vargas administration, they centered their discussions around the issue of "developmental nationalism." Those discussions have continued in one form or another until the present and have provided a large measure of continuity for modern Brazilian nationalism. It is possible to trace the evolving thought of the "developmental nationalists" through three scholarly reviews associated with them, *Cadernos do Nosso Tempo* (1953–56), *Revista Brasiliense* (1955–64), and *Revista Civilização Brasileira* (1965 to the present).

For nearly a decade (1955–64), the center of the developmental nationalist movement was the Instituto Superior de Estudos Brasileiros (Superior Institute of Brazilian Studies, or ISEB). The ISEB was established by the federal government in 1955, as an autonomous agency responsible to the Ministry of Education. The purposes of the Institute were to offer courses and conduct research on the problems of economic development. The ISEB was the outgrowth of two private study groups—the so-called Itatiaia group and the Instituto Brasileiro de Economia, Sociologia e Política (Brazilian Institute of Economics, Sociology, and Politics)—that had been formed in the early 1950's by a number of the bright young men around Vargas. During its lifetime, the ISEB sponsored seminars, courses, and lectures, and published books on philosophy, history, politics, sociology, education, and economics.

The Institute also undertook to formulate the ideological doctrine for developmental nationalism. Its members were in agreement that national planning was required to develop a vibrant economy that would be in the hands of the Brazilians themselves. They agreed that the state would have to oversee and guide such planning and development. However, they disagreed as to whether a basically socialistic or capitalistic economy would best serve Brazil's interests. That disagreement eventually split the ISEB, as it has divided the nationalist movement.

During its early years, the ISEB was largely under the control of the moderate nationalists, who believed that development could take place without the complete socialization of the economy. Their philosophical position was reflected in such works as Hélio Jaguaribe's *O Nacionalismo na Atualidade Brasileira* (Nationalism in the Brazilian Reality), Alvaro Vieira Pinto's *Consciência e Realidade Nacional* (National Consciousness and Reality), and Cândido Mendes de Almeida's *Nacionalismo e Desenvolvimento* (Nationalism and Development). Professor Jaguaribe's study in particular incensed many of the radical nationalists because it favored the use of foreign capital in the development of Petrobrás. The radicals considered the book to be *entreguista*—a word whose emotional overtones are difficult to convey in translation—advocating a "sell out" of Brazil's national resources. Heated debates and acrimonious inquiries followed the publication of the book, with the moderate nationalists defending the text and the radicals denouncing it.

In 1959, the radical nationalists, who urged state ownership of the principal industries and control of foreign investments, gained control of the ISEB, and many moderates, including Jaguaribe and Mendes de Almeida, resigned. Under the guidance of the prolific writer and ardent nationalist Nelson Werneck Sodré, the Institute increasingly used Marxist terminology, advocated more extreme positions, and intensified its political involvement. The ISEB remained a center of fervent nationalist activity until it was dissolved by the military government in 1964.

The classes of the ISEB, which were attended by military officers, civil servants, and students—that is to say, by representatives of the middle class—were small, but the nationalists had various means of reaching a wider audience. Speakers visited the major cities throughout the country to spread the views of the Institute and to recruit supporters. The ISEB also achieved some political voice in the years 1957–64 through the Frente Parlamentar Nacionalista (National Parliamentary Front, or FPN), a group of radical nationalist congressmen who worked for passage of nationalist legislation. The Institute also spoke through its weekly newspaper, *O Seminário*, which had an estimated circulation of 60,000. It maintained a close relationship with the students, supporting their various demonstrations and manifestoes.

Students, a highly idealistic, restless element in Brazilian society, have long endorsed and supported the nationalist cause. From 1937 until the military coup of 1964, the center of student agitation was the União Nacional de Estudantes (National Student Union, or UNE). The UNE was founded shortly before the advent of the Estado Novo, as an affiliated branch of the government-supported Casa do Estudante (student housing). In 1940, the UNE won its autonomy and became the voice of all university students; not long thereafter, it began to play an active political role. During World War II, the students wholeheartedly supported the Allied campaign against the European dictatorships. Soon, however, they were focusing attention on their own country, and they participated in the conspiracies of 1944–45 to remove Vargas. Through the years, the students espoused more radical causes and their goals became increasingly ambitious: they sought no less than the remaking of their country, the elimination of misery and poverty, and the achievement of national prosperity and self-respect.

By the mid-1950's, the students found that they could exert considerable power and influence. The press usually gave the young idealists a sympathetic hearing. The students became a significant pressure group that lobbied effectively for government recognition; in the early 1960's, the government heavily subsidized the UNE. In 1956, students carried out their first effective strike, when they protested the increase of streetcar fares in Rio de Janeiro. They used strikes—or the threat of them—frequently thereafter to try to bring about their demands.

The UNE allied itself with such radical nationalist organizations as the ISEB and the National Parliamentary Front. It also began to concentrate more of its attention and energy on nationalist causes. Students advocated land, tax, electoral, and educational reforms. They defended Petrobrás, which they felt was threatened by international oil interests; they championed Fidel Castro, whom they considered the fomentor of true social revolution in Latin America. They opposed the United States, which they regarded as a threat to the cause of developing nations in general and to Brazil's economic emancipation in particular. The leaders of the UNE were anti-capitalist (their stereotyped "capitalism" was reminiscent of that found in the United States or Great Britain around 1840) and pro-socialist (their equally stereotyped "socialism" was of the Saint-Simonian variety). They were generally more impressed by developments in Eastern Europe and in Cuba than in the West. Although the students were frequently described as Communist, the more suitable adjective would probably be quixotic.

In the mid-1960's, young Brazilians also began to express their feelings through the medium of music. A new generation of singers and composers abandoned the melancholic *bossa nova* for protest songs based on ethnic and folk music. The lyrics of these songs decried the hunger, misery, and social injustice in the country. After the military coup of 1964, they began to show a growing preoccupation with liberty. The single most popular theme has been the impoverished Northeast. A hit song of 1965, "Carcará," lamented the poverty and hunger of the Northeast that forced the poor to abandon their homes. In mid-song, the singer pauses to remind his listeners: "In 1950 there were two million Northeasterners living outside their native states; 10 per cent of the population of Ceará emigrated, 13 per cent of Piauí, more than 15 per cent of Bahia and 17 per cent of Alagoas." To standing-room-only audiences, the students of São Paulo's Catholic University presented the musical drama *Vida e Morte de Severino* (Life and Death of Severino), a poem of João Cabral de Melo Neto set to the music of Chico Buarque de Holanda. The poem tells of the peasant Severino, who wanders through the arid backlands of the Northeast observing unhappiness, misery, and death. At one point, during the burial scene of a peasant, the chorus sings: "This land where you lie is just the right size—not too long, not too wide. Here is your share of the *latifúndio*." Blarred forth from the ubiquitous transistor radios, protest music provided a most effective form of communication in a land where 50 per cent of the population is illiterate.

A majority of the young protesters, as well as most of the students and intellectuals, come from the middle class, which furnishes the core and the leadership of the nationalist movement. The Brazilian middle class—which comprises about 15 per cent of the total population of the country—is the most articulate segment of the population, and among its members are found the formulators of public opinion. The majority of officers in the armed forces also come from the middle class. It is the group that is most acutely aware of the restrictions imposed by the traditional oligarchy and most able to express its disapproval or resentment of the situation. It is also, potentially, the principal beneficiary of nationalist policies. The expropriation or nationalization of foreign-owned property, the encouragement of native industry, the restrictions on foreign employment, the expansion of the role of the government, and hence of the bureaucracy, all tend to redistribute income in favor of the middle class and to make new jobs available to its members, particularly among the highly educated sector. It is not surprising, therefore, that in general the middle class is nationalistic.

It is more difficult to explain the nationalism manifested by the urban working class. Vargas' economic policies and social welfare programs did bring some tangible benefits to the urban workers. Yet any monetary returns the workers may receive as a result of nationalist policies will be considerably less than those that will be enjoyed by the middle class. In fact, there are few cases to date of the workers' relative position being improved by nationalist policies. Indeed, Latin America provides several examples to the contrary, of which Bolivia and Cuba are the most obvious. There the real wages of the workers failed to rise despite the nationalist rhetoric and reform. However, it is doubtful whether the urban worker understands that nationalism will bring him little material benefits. The nationalist program seems to promise something for everyone, and so long as it consists more of talk than of action, it will no doubt continue to appeal to the working class. Vargas and Goulart, at any rate, proved that the urban worker can be roused to support the nationalist program.

Although the urban workers and middle class are clearly more concerned with urban and industrial problems than with the problems of rural areas, many members of the middle class do support land reform, partly because it will deal a heavy blow against the landowning oligarchy. What few nationalists realized—or cared to admit—was that the economic development coveted by urban dwellers was in fact unattainable if it excluded the numerically dominant rural population.

The rural classes themselves are less interested in and sympathetic to the nationalist cause. Francisco Julião, the leader of the Peasant Leagues in the Northeast during the early 1960's, believed that the peasant could not be won to nationalism so long as he was a "slave." "So far the peasant knows as his companions hunger, misery, nakedness, slavery, and death. Patriotism, loyalty to the country, is for him an immense sugar refinery where he moans like the slave for whom Nabuco did his all to set free."[8]

The statistics on rural Brazil are not comforting, in a country where 50 per cent of the arable land is in the hands of less than 2 per cent of the landowners. A few large landowners benefit from the wealth of the soil, while the large landless class—deprived of decent living conditions, education, medical aid, and suffering from malnutrition—eke out a miserable existence. The nationalists, according to Julião, had an obligation to lead the peasants into the mainstream of the national life.

These views were shared by another Pernambucan, Miguel Arraes, who carried his convictions into the political arena. Campaigning on a nationalist platform in 1962, he was elected governor of Pernambuco, the key state of the agricultural Northeast. As governor, he devoted the major share of his attention to rural problems. In mid-1963, in the presence of President Goulart and 100,000 workers, he attacked the Alliance for Progress as a ploy of the United States to perpetuate the status quo, and called for basic land reform:

Our rich daily become richer, while each sunrise brings new misery to our poor. When the poor decide to unite and thus gain some strength, the only immediate reaction, until very recently, was the most inhumane political violence. That violence coldly assassinated, still assassinates, rural leaders whose only crime is to struggle to organize agrarian labor and to advocate agrarian reform. The large landowners, enjoying centuries-old privileges, have done everything, and will still do much, to try to prevent or to discredit the land reform that the people demand and begin to make. For the large landowners, every means and every resource are good and legitimate as long as they serve to maintain their privileges. Therefore, one sees their desperation here in Pernambuco upon understanding that they no longer own the government and can no longer count on the police for arbitrary action and violence as they did in the past. Therefore, one sees their close alliance with imperialism in order to be better able to dominate this land economically and politically. . . . . We must urgently plan and execute our land reform so desired by the rural masses. What we have done until now is very little, almost nothing, in comparison to the great task ahead.[9]

His audience cheered those words. Combated by the powerful influence of the entrenched landowning oligarchy, Julião and Arraes were able to arouse—although only to a limited degree—the neglected rural masses of the Northeast to unite in favor of basic reforms.

Specific issues, then, have been the key to enlisting support for the nationalist cause. The abstract concept of nationalism elicits a limited response. At any rate, there is no undisputed nationalist doctrine but only a common consensus of what nationalism implies. San Tiago Dantas has commented on how this nationalist consensus was arrived at: "The attitudes . . . revealed an internal consistency which permitted the unification around a central philosophy of conduct. That does not mean that its elaboration has been empirical or casual. In the origin of each action, there was one constant present: the exclusive consideration of the interests of Brazil."[10]

Nor is there a nationalist party in Brazil; the nationalist cause cuts across party lines. In fact, over the years, various interparty organizations—such as the National Liberation Front, the Popular Mobilization Front, and the Nationalist Parliamentary Front—have sprung up to defend Petrobrás, encourage industrialization, advocate an independent foreign policy, and support other nationalist causes. The most important of these was the Nationalist Parliamentary Front, whose membership was estimated at one time to include approximately eighty deputies and senators of the federal congress. Most of these were members of the Brazilian Labor Party, but at one time or another during its seven years of activity, the Front included representatives from the two other major parties as well as from some of the eleven minor parties. During the Goulart administration, Sérgio Magalhães headed the Front, although such ultranationalist congressmen as Leonel Brizzola, Paulo de Tarso, Neiva Moreira, and Temperani Pereira often dominated it.

Political labels have never been very significant in Brazil, however. Politicians switch parties with remarkable agility, swinging from right to left, like San Tiago Dantas, or from left to right, like Luís Alberto Bahia, and continuing to be ardent nationalists. They have also on occasion adopted one, or several, of the nationalist attitudes, yielding to expediency or demagoguery to bolster their own positions.

The number of nationalist activists remains small in proportion to the total population. A poll taken in 1960–61 by the Instituto de Estudos Sociais e Econômicos (Institute of Social and Economic Studies) sought out the "avowed nationalists"—in the poll's definition, "those who know about 'nationalism' and agree with the 'nationalists' "—and found they totaled only 7 per cent of the urban, and 1 per cent of the rural, population. A majority of the "avowed nationalists" were male, university-educated, middle-class residents of Brazil's large cities. The poll also revealed that the nationalist minority constituted the most vocal element and provided much of the political leadership in Brazil; their influence has been far greater than their numbers. In the same poll, when federal legislators were asked if they considered themselves "nationalists," 89 per cent replied in the affirmative, 2 per cent in the negative, and 9 per cent either qualified their responses or had no opinion.[11] The nationalists are the first to admit that the masses do not understand nationalism. But, they add, there exists an immense reservoir of national sentiment, waiting to be tapped. As proof, they point to the profound feelings that the Petrobrás campaign aroused in the masses. Under the proper stimulus, they feel, it is possible vastly to expand nationalist support to include a majority of the population.

The psychological setting for popular nationalism has also improved as Brazilians have seen their achievements and talents receive international recognition. During the 1950's and 1960's, as they began to exert a positive influence on the world around them, they experienced a rapid and steady growth of national pride. When the Brazilian soccer team won the world championship in 1958, and again in 1962, the victories became occasions for national holidays, celebrated with dancing in the streets and typical Brazilian exuberance. Pelé, the adored soccer ace, was the talk of the nation. Brazil thrilled to other athletic victories, such as that of tennis star Maria Bueno, who won the Wimbledon women's singles championship in 1960. Brazilian beauty was also heralded abroad; there was hardly a Miss World or a Miss Universe contest that did not include a Miss Brazil among the finalists. The news media gave these pageants detailed coverage, and in 1963, when Miss Brazil emerged as Miss Universe, the nation rejoiced.

Brazilian music, art, and literature also burst their national frontiers. The works of the composer Villa-Lobos were already known in concert halls around the world. Now, the sound of the *bossa nova* was heard in Europe and the United States. Musicians such as João Gilberto, Antônio Carlos Jobim, Sérgio Mendes, and Edú Lôbo played before international audiences. "The Girl from Ipanema" became a hit song in the United States. The fledgling movie industry achieved success in 1963, when *Pagador de Promessas* (The Keeper of Promises) received awards at both the Cannes and San Francisco film festivals. The imaginative architecture of Brasília excited comment and admiration around the world, and the international press devoted considerable attention to the emergence of the bold new capital city in the Brazilian interior.

Brazilian literature for the first time received worldwide recognition, as the works of Graciliano Ramos, José Lins do

Rêgo, Erico Veríssimo, Guimarães Rosa, and Jorge Amado were translated into many languages. Amado's novel *Gabriela, Clove and Cinnamon* became a best-seller in the United States. The major novels of Machado de Assis were published in English, together with critical studies of his work. Institutes of Brazilian studies were established in the United States, Japan, and a number of European nations, and chairs in Brazilian studies were set up at the major universities in these countries. The result of the international recognition accorded Brazilian achievements in the past two decades has been the shedding of former inferiority complexes, and the growth of national pride. Nebulous as it might be, that pride has contributed significantly to the growth of contemporary nationalism.

The high point of nationalist agitation was reached in early 1964. President Goulart was increasingly turning to the nationalists for support and catering to their wishes. He showed himself willing to mouth nationalist phrases, and on occasion demonstrated that he could rouse the masses to fever pitch. (Goulart's personal actions sometimes belied his words, however. At the same time that he was advocating land reform, he was buying up millions of acres of land, to become one of the largest landowners in the nation.)

On March 13, 1964, Goulart spoke at a lively rally whose most conspicuous sponsor was the coordinating directorate of unions, the General Labor Command, strongly suspected of being under Communist influence, if not control. That speech offered the first public indication that Goulart was willing to implement the program advocated by the radical nationalists. Before a crowd of 150,000 he signed a decree nationalizing private oil refineries and another initiating a modest land reform program. He promised more decrees in the near future.

The country was clearly in a state of unrest. The public was concerned over the unbridled inflation and the rising cost of living. Budget deficits increased; government income met only 75 per cent of the expenses. The chaotic financial situation, coupled with political uncertainty, aroused the concern of all responsible elements of society. The military waited anxiously in the wings, unhappy over the situation but still unwilling to march onto the political stage. Goulart had carefully cultivated the officers, but in his flight into demagoguery he found it tempting to appeal directly to the enlisted men. When three thousand sailors and marines rebelled against their anti-Goulart officers on March 25, the President let it be known that they would receive an amnesty. On the night of March 30, the President spoke before a meeting of sergeants in Rio de Janeiro. The nationally televised speech was a bitter attack on the military hierarchy and on discipline and order in general. The officers reacted at once. Those of predominantly rightist tendencies, as well as those who until that moment were undecided, took up the challenge and overthrew their commander in chief on the grounds that he was either a Communist or under Communist control. A large segment of the population, apprehensive over the accelerating inflation and perpetual government crises, took to the streets to support the military move.

The government was deserted on every side. The nationalists—partly because they understood the hopelessness of the situation, partly because they had never fully trusted the erratic President—unemotionally watched Goulart fall. Only a small number of labor leaders, politicians, and intellectuals spoke out to defend their President. A few isolated calls for the people to rush to the barricades were met with deafening silence. Truly a haunting hush accompanied Goulart on his flight from Rio de Janeiro to Brasília, from there to Pôrto Alegre, and finally, on April 4, into Uruguay from whence he had come to assume the presidency during the crisis of September, 1961. But on April 1, the military had already taken control of the government.

The nationalists had had reservations about Goulart, but they were totally unprepared for what was to follow. The new military government of President Marshal Humberto Castelo Branco purged Congress of all unfriendly elements; packed the Supreme Court; imposed press censorship; took away the political rights of hundreds of Brazilians (including such notable figures as economist Celso Furtado, architect Oscar Niemeyer, and former presidents Kubitschek and Quadros); disbanded the existing political parties and created official government and opposition parties; annulled state elections and removed state governors from office; and imposed military justice on civilians. Those actions struck a stunning blow against the growth of democracy in Brazil. In the process, the nationalists found themselves dispossessed of their positions and power and discredited by the ruling military hierarchy.

Overnight, the situation of the nationalists had changed. From their defensive position, they sought to find the cause of their misfortune. Their attention was quickly fixed on their old bogeyman, the United States. The U.S. government and press had been openly hostile to Goulart and critical of nationalist attitudes and legislation, such as the profits remission law. President Johnson made no effort to disguise his pleasure over the fall of the Goulart government. He telegraphed his congratulations within hours after the military's seizure of power (even before a cabinet had been formed) and expressed his admiration for the way the Brazilians had settled the matter "within the framework of constitutional democracy and without civil strife." Washington also stepped up its economic aid to the military government. The nationalists saw an evil conspiracy in those events, and accused the United States of cooperating in the overthrow of Goulart and the setting up of a military dictatorship. A whole body of nationalist literature on the subject sprang up, the best known of which is Edmar Morel's *O Golpe Começou em Washington* (The Coup Originated in Washington).

The nationalists found some basis for their accusation that the United States approved the military plotting and eventual *coup d'état* in remarks made by Thomas C. Mann, Assistant Secretary of State for Inter-American Affairs. In a closed session with U.S. ambassadors to Latin America in mid-March, 1964, Mann had outlined the policy the Johnson administration intended to follow in Latin America. His remarks were reported in *The New York Times* of March 19, 1964, under the heading "U.S. May Abandon Effort to Deter Latin Dictators." According to Secretary Mann, the United States would no longer seek to punish military juntas for overthrowing democratic regimes. Mann also confessed that he had "difficulties in distinguishing" between General Alfredo Stroessner (the military dictator of Paraguay) and President Adolfo López Mateos (the democratically elected civilian president of Mexico). To Mann, apparently, one chief of state was the same as another, regardless of how he came to power or how he exercised it. The fact that Mann's comments were made less than two weeks before the military coup in Brazil increased the suspicions of the nationalists.

Then in November, 1966, a report appeared in *Newsweek* magazine that made Brazilian nationalists nod their heads in I-told-you-so fashion. *Newsweek* reported:

[In Brazil] Washington shrewdly assigned bustling fast-talking Brig. Gen. Vernon A. Walters to Rio de Janeiro as military attaché two years before the coup. A brilliant linguist, Walters had served as liaison officer with the Brazilian Expeditionary Force in Italy in World War II, and in Rio de Janeiro he immediately renewed his warm friendship with the Brazilian brass. As Brazil's erratic President Goulart swung farther and farther left, Walters became the confidante of the military plotters against Goulart and finally encouraged Gen. Humberto

Castelo Branco, who had been his roommate in Italy, to take power. A week before the coup, Walters wired full details of its organization to Washington and the day after Castelo Branco was inaugurated as President, lunched with him privately in the Presidential Palace.

Since that time, Walters has become one of the new Brazilian Government's most enthusiastic and influential boosters. His manifesto entitled "Why Brazil Is Different," which argues against U.S. arms ceilings for Latin America (and especially Brazil), has circulated widely in the State Department and the Pentagon. And while Walters insists that he leaves arms negotiations up to the Rio MAP (Military Assistance Program) mission, which numbers more than 100 men, the fact remains that Brazil upped its purchase of U.S. arms from $2.5 million in 1965 to $12 million in 1966, making it one of Latin America's biggest buyers of U.S. weapons.

Under questioning, U.S. officials revealed last week that part of this $12 million is being spent on 100 M-41 tanks, presumably to maintain internal security. Whether tanks are really necessary for this purpose is arguable.[12]

These charges by a responsible American news magazine even went beyond those of Edmar Morel. The nationalists clamored for an explanation. The United States Embassy in Rio denied any veracity in the *Newsweek* account. At this point, Carlos Lacerda, who during his career has espoused every political view from the far left to the far right, lent his authority and prestige to the nationalist cause by calling for a clarification of the *Newsweek* report.[13] The nationalist case against the United States was certainly strengthened by such accounts in the American press. The nationalists were able to convince large segments of the population that the United States had intervened, and thereby enlarged the reservoir of anti-Yankee sentiment, which they will doubtless tap in the future.

The few officers who dominated the new military government were unsympathetic to the nationalist cause. This was a new development in Brazilian political life. Since it over-

threw the monarchy in 1889—the event that marked its en-
trance onto the political stage—the military had been regarded, and regarded itself, as the major force of national
unity and the guardian of nationality. In the last analysis, the
military was the only truly effective institution that was national in both scope and organization. The military carefully
wielded the *poder moderador*, the moderative power once exercised by the emperors, to balance the variety of political elements for the benefit of the nation. In 1930, 1945, 1954, 1955,
and 1961, the military stepped into politics long enough to
effect a change or balance the political scales. The military
was proud of its record, particularly in comparison with that of
its counterparts in Spanish-speaking America. On the whole,
the military did a respectable job and on more than one occasion protected and even encouraged democracy. However,
after the 1964 coup, the military followed a new path. The
officers did not rebalance the political structure and then
retire, leaving politics to the civilians. Contrary to past prac-
tice, they remained in power and became involved in partisan political struggles. Once having done so, the military
was no longer a unifying force. And as it was no longer a
unifying force, neither was it a unified force.

The military in Brazil in 1964 was split into two factions.
One was strongly nationalistic. For some time the nationalistic officers rallied around Marshal Henrique Teixeira Lott. A
career military officer, Lott had political ambitions; he ran
for the presidency in 1960 and for the governorship of Guanabara in 1965 (before being disqualified on a technicality),
but both times as a citizen and not as a marshal. "I resent the
insinuations that I am a military candidate," he remarked in
1960.[14] In the mid-1950's, Lott belonged to the Movimento
Militar Constitucionalista (Constitutionalist Military Movement). In November, 1955, he led the effort to ensure that
constitutionally elected President Kubitschek assume office.
In 1961, he supported the elevation of Vice President Gou-

lart to the presidency. Lott has called nationalism "the only position compatible with dignity and the only arm of emancipation for the country."[15] He called for "the adoption of a nationalist orientation as a solution for Brazilian problems."[16] He had favored extending the vote to illiterates, a nationalist political goal considered capable of breaking the hold of the oligarchy, and limiting profit remittances abroad.

Support for nationalism within the military seems to have a firm base. In a 1966 poll of the military, 47 per cent of the officers questioned declared themselves unreservedly as nationalists; another 27 per cent listed themselves as moderate nationalists; only 5 per cent were "opposed" to nationalism.[17] It would be difficult to ascertain exactly what this emotionally charged word meant to the officers questioned, however. A senior officer, General Pery Bevilacqua, has defined nationalism as follows: "Above all, nationalism is a patriotic attitude of vigilance over and defense of the fundamental interests of the country. . . . It is the national conscience of the economic development of Brazil. Our nationalism is a genuinely Brazilian nationalism, which begins and ends in Brazil, concerned exclusively with the interest and well-being of Brazil."[18]

It is not certain whether all those who claimed in the poll to be nationalists would agree with even this mild definition. One can perhaps get a better feeling for the breadth of nationalist support among the military by examining their stands on various issues. The officers almost unanimously supported the creation of Petrobrás. Most of them favor industrialization, although there is a considerable difference of opinion over the means to achieve that end. On the question of land reform, there is considerable variance of opinion. On matters of foreign policy, the rifts are deep and on political questions even deeper. Those officers who will be called nationalists hereafter in the text are those who generally support industrialization, modernization, an independent foreign policy, and nonparticipation of the military in politics. Indications are—as suggested by the 1966 poll—that the number of nationalist officers is high.

The nationalist officers desire to restore the military to its traditional and historic role as the *poder moderador*. General Estévão Leitão de Carvalho forcefully argued this idea in his book *Dever Militar e Política Partidária* (Military Duty and Partisan Politics). In an interview in 1966, Rear Admiral Norton D. Boiteux was asked whether it was true that total power in Brazil rested in the hands of the military. He replied: "Effectively and absolutely all power is in the hands of the military. I hope that the good officers will meditate on this, will reconsider, and will return with humility and patriotism to the only position [defenders of the nation] that the Constitution assigns to them."[19]

The leadership in the Brazilian government since April 1, 1964, has come from the opposite faction in the military, the one that fears nationalism and opposes it. Curiously, many of these leaders were the *tenentes* of a generation ago, that is, they were once avant-garde nationalists.

Marshal Castelo Branco evidenced a strong suspicion of all nationalists. He repeatedly warned his compatriots to beware of "false nationalists," a name he liberally applied to those from whom he had seized power.[20] He defined "false nationalists" as those "irresponsible" individuals "who want to consume and not to save, who speak of development of the vast interior but who never abandon the comfort of the cities, who steadfastly defend privileges and tenaciously refuse duties, who clamor for government investments but also demand lower taxes and higher salaries, who criticize foreign capital, but offer no solution to increase national savings."[21]

Castelo Branco frequently quoted from the writings of Gustavo Corção, one of the few writers who condemned nationalism during the 1956–64 period. Corção regarded na-

tionalism as a form of collective madness. He believed that
nationalist policies stifled private initiative and would inevitably lead either to totalitarianism or to Communism. He
criticized the nationalism of both Plínio Salgado and Getúlio
Vargas. "To exalt Brazil is not necessarily good," he said, "nationalism in reality destroys the nation."[22] Although Corção
made some valid points—exaggerated nationalism can be
a destructive rather than a constructive force—he was out of
touch with the emotionalism prevalent in an underdeveloped
country eager for reform and progress.

Castelo Branco and the officers supporting him tended to
equate nationalism with Communism. They had received
their advanced military instruction at the Escola Superior de
Guerra (Superior War College), founded in 1949 to give advanced courses on national defense to senior military officers
and distinguished civilians. Propagating an almost patho-
logical brand of anti-Communism, the College warned
against the alliance of Communists and nationalists. Its grad-
uates were soon equating the two. As evidenced in an article
in *O Jornal* of Rio de Janeiro in 1961, the two were also
being linked together in public discussion,[23] and this tendency increased during the Goulart administration. This con-
fusion resulted from the fact that the Communists usually
supported at least part of the program put forth by the nationalists. Both, for example, advocated land reform, decried
U.S. imperialism, and sought to limit foreign economic pene-
tration. Furthermore, most of the nationalist leadership stood
to the left of political center and in their speeches and writings
tended to employ a Marxist vocabulary. In refutation of this
view, in 1962, General Bevilacqua pointed out the danger of
confusing Communism and nationalism,[24] thus upholding the
point of view taken years earlier by the journalist Carlos Maul,
who affirmed: "Nationalism is the primary enemy of Communism."[25]

The military government took firm steps to disestablish

nationalist institutions and to revoke nationalist legislation. Both the Superior Institute of Brazilian Studies and the National Student Union were disbanded. Their leaders were charged with subversion and tried by Military Courts of Inquiry, which handed down sentences ranging from the cancellation of fellowships to the suspension of political rights. On August 29, 1964, the government repealed the profits remittance law, over the vehement protests of the nationalists, who succeeded in delaying the enabling legislation until February 18, 1965. The repeal of the law increased the rift between the nationalists and the Castelo Branco government, and also accentuated the anti-Americanism of the former, who saw in the government's actions the heavy hand of Washington. The government put up for sale the Fábrica Nacional de Motores (National Motor Industry), another pride of the nationalists, opposed the establishment of a state petrochemical industry, and even began to tamper with Petrobrás, favoring cooperation with foreign oil companies. New concessions were made to a variety of foreign companies, including the Hanna Mining Corporation, the *bête noire* of the nationalists.

In foreign policy, the Brazilian government made a complete about face. The Castelo Branco government viewed the international scene as a struggle between East and West, in which there could be no neutral position. Castelo Branco made it unmistakably clear that Brazil was allied with the West in its struggle to protect the values threatened by the Soviet bloc. He committed Brazil to closer relations with the United States and to the other Latin American countries, and de-emphasized relations with the countries of Africa, Asia, and the Communist nations.

In a major foreign policy speech on November 21, 1966, Foreign Minister Juracy Magalhães, a former Ambassador to the United States, reiterated the guidelines set forth by the President. He acknowledged the United States as the "unquestioned leader of the free world" and the "principal guardian of the fundamental values of our civilization." As an "ally for over 140 years," the United States was Brazil's best customer, largest investor, and foremost source of technical knowledge. Therefore, relations between the two countries should be especially intimate. The Foreign Minister regarded the Western hemisphere as the natural sphere for Brazilian action. In discussing relations with other American republics, he emphasized the themes of hemispheric unity, collective security, and economic solidarity. He made only passing mention of relations with the non-Western world.

The new military government broke off diplomatic relations with Cuba, and voted against the seating of Communist China in the United Nations. President Castelo Branco expressed his government's solidarity with the U.S. position in Viet-Nam. All of these diplomatic positions represented complete reversals of policy. Brazilian troops also took part in the intervention in the Dominican Republic in 1965, a decision defended by one officer in the following words:

> The Armed Forces brilliantly stopped Communism from taking over Brazil. Another brilliant example is their participation in the Dominican Republic in the operation initiated by the American Marines, where they also stopped Communism from taking over the country.[26]

The Castelo Branco government supported the controversial Inter-American Peace Force, and Foreign Minister Magalhães visited a number of South American capitals to urge support for the force.

As a result of their foreign and domestic policies, Castelo Branco and his supporters were labeled "anti-nationalists" by the nationalists. They were felt to be more concerned with questions of security, stability, sound financial practices, and balanced budgets than with reform, industrialization, and modernization. The nationalists charged that the military government's policies were detrimental to Brazil's development. Carlos Lacerda, one of the instigators of the April coup, accused the military government of being "not infrequently linked with interests foreign to those of the nation."[27] A nationalist editor, Hélio Fernandes, argued that the defeat of nationalism—"this nationalism latent and dominant within the Brazilian people"—meant the arrest of development. He reasoned that "without nationalism there is no development, without development there is no progress, without progress it is impossible to enrich the nation, and if the nation remains poor so do all its citizens."[28] The nationalist reasons for opposing the economic policies of the military government were well summed up in these remarks by federal deputy Doutel de Andrade:

> I judge the present economic and financial policies of the Castelo Branco government as wretched, anti-national, retrograde, and insensible to popular anxieties. The advance of foreign interests into basic sectors of our industrial production has never been so complete. The hysterical fixation on monetary policies, the slavish fulfillment of plans drawn up abroad are causing stagnation; it is causing misery to the middle class; it is transforming the working masses into virtual pariahs who live a tragic day-to-day existence not knowing where their next meal will come from. Besides that, inflation continues and the scarcity of goods is alarming. But some, protected by the government and associated with foreign interests, fill their pockets. The International Monetary Fund and the [U.S.] Department of State have already given examples, such as Argentina, of their ability to strangle a national economy when they place it under their rigid planning. What is good for the trusts of the United States is always bad for the nations in the process of emancipation because the interests of the two are antagonistic.
>
> For these reasons, I find the position taken toward foreign capital by the present government to be negative. I look with patriotic indignation on the progressive domination of our industries and the criminal control of our primary materials by foreign groups which do not even need to invest heavily in our nation in order to achieve their ends. The manipulation of a

good part of the national savings by the investment companies linked to foreign groups in the exterior permits, and often the Brazilian government itself encourages, that they constantly control more and become a kind of fifth column which undermines national resistance and places Brazil and its people in the infamous position of a colony. The pharmaceutical, petrochemical, automotive, and metallurgic industries, and so many others of strategic importance, are today in the hands of either great trusts or foreign corporations.[29]

Criticism of the military government's policies has not come solely from the hard-core nationalists. The statistics on living costs and business stagnation indicate that the government may face opposition from the general public as well. In 1965, the wage earner lost 14 per cent of his purchasing power; in 1966, 22 per cent. In 1967, the government, in alliance with business interests, again kept wage increases below consumer price rises. It is true that the government, through draconic measures, succeeded in slowing down the rate of inflation, perhaps by as much as one-third in 1967. However, this was achieved at the expense of further devaluation of the currency and a recession marked by widespread business failures and lower productivity. Business interests criticized the government for keeping too tight a rein on the economy; wage earners blamed it for the decline in purchasing power. The government is the military, and thus for the first time the people are assuming firm anti-military attitudes.

The nationalist military officers are distressed to see the entire military establishment discredited. "What is so very grave is that the Brazilian people can conclude that the armed forces are responsible for all those acts which at this time interrupt the development of the country by slowing down its economic emancipation," Marshal Lott remarked.[30] Two distinguished civilians, Bishop Jorge Marcos de Oliveira and federal deputy Hermógenes Príncipe, both concluded that the forebodings Lott expressed have a solid base in reality.[31] Admiral Boiteux stated that "it is an illusion of the

military to think that they are admired by the civilian population."[32] He believed instead that the majority of civilians
were afraid of the military. The remedy for this declining
popularity, according to General Olímpio Mourão Filho, is
for the military to get out of politics and stay out.[33]

Not all the military nationalists are prepared to forego the
temptation to hold on to political power, however. A small
but vocal wing, occupying a position to the far right of Castelo Branco, has advocated "saving" Brazil through the im-
position of a rigid, military dictatorship of the classic *caudillo*
type. Known as the *linha dura* ("hard line"), this group differs
diametrically from the Lott supporters on the question of the
military's participation in politics. As fervent nationalists,
however, they condemn "foreign pillaging" and are strongly
xenophobic and chauvinistic.

With the inauguration of Marshal Artur da Costa e Silva
as President, on March 15, 1967, the nationalists felt encouraged that they might be able to regain at least a modicum
of their former influence. *Ultima Hora*, a leftist, nationalist
newspaper, expressed those hopes in its front-page headline
"Costa Will Return Brazil to the Brazilians."[34] The press also
predicted that Costa e Silva would be attentive to the pleas
of the national business community, which, jealous of the
privileges bestowed on foreigners under Castelo Branco, had
been resorting to some of the traditional nationalist arguments against foreign capital.[35]

The new President has seemed more inclined to support
the nationalist causes of industrialization, economic development, and an independent foreign policy than was his predecessor. The questions of a balanced budget, sound financial
practices, and "purification" of the body politic concern
him less. Whether out of political conviction or simply because he is of a more easygoing nature, Costa e Silva has permitted a wider latitude of action in Brazilian political life.
The death of Castelo Branco in an air accident in July, 1967,

doubtless gave him greater freedom of maneuverability than he had enjoyed previously. Some months thereafter, the government announced that it had been "restudying" the agreement signed by Castelo Branco with the United States to guarantee American investments in Brazil. The new government also enacted regulations to prohibit investment by foreign capitalists in the new petrochemical industry.

In foreign affairs, the Costa e Silva government has shown increasing flexibility and independence. In his first major foreign policy pronouncement, the new President, after ritually evoking the name of Rio-Branco, advocated the use of diplomacy to further national development:

> I desire to mobilize our diplomacy for economic goals so as to ensure the necessary external collaboration for the acceleration of our development. . . . The foreign policy of my government will reflect fully our just aspirations for economic and social progress, our disapproval of backwardness, ignorance, sickness, and misery—in short, our decision to develop intensively our country.[36]

Foreign Minister José de Magalhães Pinto has spoken of a foreign policy in which Brazil is aligned only with Brazil. He reversed the position of his predecessor, Juracy Magalhães, with regard to the Inter-American Peace Force. In early October, 1967, he stated that Brazil had abandoned definitively the idea of a hemispheric police force—"the long and strong arm of United States policy in Latin America to preserve the imperial status quo," to use the description of one nationalist.[37] The Foreign Minister reasserted Brazil's traditional concept of nonintervention in other nations.

But neither those faint overtures to the nationalists nor a vigilant system of censorship can still all criticism of the military government. The persistent critic Carlos Lacerda proved to be one of its shrillest challengers. At the end of 1967, in a commencement address before law school students at the

Catholic University in Porto Alegre, Lacerda launched his strongest attack against the military government.

> The military have done almost nothing of value in the last years. They have sterilized public life. They have only consolidated the mistakes of the past. They cannot substitute for the will of the people. They are the victims of ambition.[38]

He told the students to organize against the dictatorship, to agitate for the restoration of full political rights for all Brazilians, and "to take your proper place again and put in your claims for what is rightfully yours." His challenge to the students to reassume their role as agitators, his sharp criticism of the United States, and his call for national development were all arguments taken from the nationalist notebook and were further proof that nationalism is the strongest force opposing the present military government.

After a cold winter, the nationalists are hopeful of a thaw and a chance to regain some of their former influence. Yet, the oft-repeated charge that nationalism and Communism are related hovers in the background and forces the nationalists to move with the greatest caution. Only the courageous express those nationalistic sentiments so much in vogue in the decade before April, 1964. Today, nationalism remains on the defensive. It would seem that the military coup of 1964 has at least temporarily diverted Brazilian nationalism from that pattern of continuous—if spasmodic—growth that began with the nativism of several centuries ago.

7. The Reckoning

The mature nationalism of twentieth-century Brazil differs markedly from its timid infancy in the colonial period and awkward adolescence in the nineteenth century. Principally it is more dynamic, positive, and aggressive. It is true that the intellectuals still express nationalist sentiments, that the city continues to be the center of nationalist expression, and that nationalism is still strongly xenophobic. These are the enduring characteristics of Brazilian nationalism. But in the twentieth century, as the base of nationalist support expanded, as the state assumed greater responsibility for leadership in nationalist causes (as it did between 1930 and 1964), and as development became the primary emphasis of nationalism, the enduring characteristics—combined with or modified by the newer trends—assumed less importance than they had in the past. Nationalism emerged in twentieth-century Brazil as both a doctrine and a force to renovate the country.

Today, Brazilian nationalism is as much preoccupied with the possibilities of the future as it used to be absorbed in tracing its roots in the past. In earlier times, the nationalists (or the nativists) expended their energy glorifying the potential wealth and natural beauty of their land, and the valor of their forebears. Contemporary nationalists have not forgotten their surroundings or the past, but they have broadened their vision to include the future as well. Not only do they boast of a glorious past, as did Afonso Celso, but—as exemplified in the writings of Cândido Mendes de Almeida

—they agitate for and predict a promising future, to which development is the key. In recent decades, the nationalists have become the strongest force encouraging development. They foresee an industrialized future in which the structures and patterns of the twentieth century will replace those of the colonial past.

Nationalism presently has two major goals: first, to achieve Brazil's economic independence through industrialization and control of foreign capital and, second, to gain status for Brazil as a world power. Both objectives reflect the confidence Brazilians began to feel at the opening of the twentieth century. At that time, the Baron of Rio-Branco, as Minister of Foreign Relations, initiated his program of national aggrandizement and international leadership—still the guidelines for Brazilian foreign policy. The two world wars, the Depression, and the administrations of Getúlio Vargas launched Brazil on the road to industrialization, along which it now speeds forward. For the past three decades, the nationalists have concentrated their energy and talents on promoting attainment of these two goals.

The intrusion of the military into the government on April 1, 1964, complicated and, at least temporarily, altered the growth of nationalism in Brazil. The military have contributed to the development of Brazilian nationalism over the years, and on occasion, they have successfully played the role of guardian of national sentiment. There was a time—notably during the Old Republic—when the military could presume to speak for a politically immature and unsophisticated republic. The increase of political maturity, as evidenced by the development of political parties and of an informed public opinion, has made that function unnecessary and even unacceptable. When the military moved to prevent the constitutional accession of Vice President João Goulart to the presidency in 1961, the nation reacted unfavorably—as evidenced by the press, speeches in Congress, and public demonstrations—and the military retreated. The public was clearly unwilling to give the generals carte blanche to exercise the *poder moderador*. It is evident that the military today are no longer regarded as the embodiment of nationality. Furthermore, as we have seen, the officers themselves are seriously divided over the issue of nationalism.

This curious development brings us face to face with the situation in present-day Brazil. When the military overthrew President Goulart on April 1, 1964, they had the sympathy and probably the support of the majority of their compatriots. Goulart had succeeded in discrediting himself; the *coup d'état* was therefore unopposed. But in 1964, the military did not step aside once the President was deposed. Clearly, the officers were not simply wielding the traditional, if extra-constitutional, *poder moderador* to restore the political balance. This time they were intervening to grasp political control for themselves. They entrusted the presidency to one of their ranking officers, purged the Congress, and packed the Supreme Court. In all but name, the government became a military dictatorship.

Within the larger context of twentieth-century Brazilian history, the present military government counters three well-established trends. First, military dictatorship is contrary to the Brazilian tradition of civilian control of government. Because there was no prolonged war of independence in Portuguese America, the military was slower to develop in Brazil than in Spanish America. It was not until the War of the Triple Alliance (1865–70) that the Brazilian military emerged as a strong institution. In 1889, they first interfered in politics, overthrowing the Emperor and proclaiming the republic. Until a new constitution was promulgated in 1891, Brazil was under military rule. The government then slowly reverted to civilians, a transfer that was completed by 1894. Although the military stepped in again in 1930, 1945, 1954, 1955, and 1961, the officers did not assume political direction of the nation until 1964. At that time, they became involved in both politics and partisan struggles, thus abdicating both their moderating power and their role as champions of national unity. They broke the tradition of civilian rule— a proud tradition of Brazilians, who have favorably compared their history with that of the Spanish-speaking republics. Brazilian voters expressed their displeasure with their new military government in the last free elections, in 1965, when the government's candidates lost nine of eleven contests for state governor. The military government responded by substituting legislative for popular election of governors. As the military government continues, the prestige of the armed forces declines proportionately.

Secondly, the implantation of military dictatorship in Brazil reverses the twentieth-century trend toward increased democracy. During the Old Republic, there was a gradual broadening of the electorate. Vargas aroused the interest of the literate proletariat in government and gave it a limited role to play. His overthrow in 1945 marked the opening of a period of intense democratization. Three nationwide political parties—the Social Democratic Party (PSD), Brazilian Labor Party (PTB), and National Democratic Union (UDN)—took shape and soon contributed significantly to the democratization process. Elections were regarded generally as being fair and honest, and the nation abided by the results. A sense of political sportsmanship developed within the give and take of partisan politics. It is true that illiterates remained disfranchised, but as the literacy rate slowly rose so did the number of Brazilians participating in the elections. In the 1955 presidential elections, for example, 9 million voters went to the polls; the population had doubled since the 1930 elections, but the number of eligible voters had multiplied tenfold. The steady and rapid growth of the electorate is evident in the official voting statistics for the years from 1945 through 1960: 5.9 million citizens voted in 1945; 7.9 million, in 1950; 8.6 million, in 1955; and 11.7 million, in 1960. About 13 per cent of the population voted in 1945, approximately 19 per cent in 1960. The rate of increase in the number of voters has risen steadily by about 20 per cent every four years. The Supreme Court, traditionally weak in Latin America, also began to assert its independence and to contribute to the democratization process. Complete freedom of speech and of expression was enjoyed. The 1964 *coup d'état* halted those salutary trends. The military government in every way has canceled the hard-won gains of democracy in Brazil.

Finally, the military dictatorship has made every effort to discredit nationalism as a concept and to suppress it as a force. That nationalism has deep roots in the Brazilian past and that it is the strongest force behind the current demands for change are two of the chief points made in this study. This author agrees with most students of Latin American nationalism that it is the single strongest force at work in the hemisphere south of the Rio Grande. Yet, the Brazilian military have defied this potent force and through their actions have put it on the defensive.

Although the military government has attached the adjective "revolutionary" to its name, events since April 1, 1964, have shown that it is not even a *reform* government, much less a *revolutionary* one. Rather, events seem to indicate that the military sought power both for its own sake and also to prevent change. If it so desired, this military government could use its absolute powers to promulgate and enforce land reform and to extend the vote to the illiterate. Instead, it has disbanded political parties, deprived its opponents of the vote and of other civil rights, and perverted the Supreme Court. It prefers to strengthen the currency and to impose fiscal disciplines that exclusively benefit the business community, domestic and foreign, and strengthen the dominant elite. Witness to the military government's lack of genuine concern for the well-being of the populace in general is the fact that since it took power the cost of living has risen more than 100 per cent, while wage increases have been held to two-thirds of that figure. Indications are, therefore, that the military government will not undertake the essential basic reforms that could free Brazil from its past and project it into the future.

At the present, then, there is neither an emperor, a Vargas, nor the military to direct nationalism. The nationalist movement flounders leaderless. Consequently, it is a diffuse force today, less potent than it was in the 1930–64 period. The aggressive nationalism, so characteristic of the post-imperial era, has been muted—at least for the moment.

But nationalism is too potent a force, too popular a rallying cry, to be suppressed for long. In the opinion of one observant visitor to South America, Arnold Toynbee, "Nationalism has, indeed, become a more potent religion than Christianity."[1] The Brazilians have been increasingly prone to worship at its altar. Nationalism is still a chief topic of conversation among the intellectuals, and the quantity of literature being published on the subject is impressive. But what is of greater significance is that over the past twenty years nationalism has become a doctrine increasingly appealing to larger and larger segments of the population. The economy is no longer a simple extractive one. Profound industrialization has taken place, and the society is becoming increasingly modernized. The nation has showed that it can exercise greater independence in its international relations. The population in general is becoming aware of these advancements, proud of them, and enticed by the mystique of a greater Brazil that will provide a more decent life for all. There is reason to believe that, after the present military interlude, nationalism will reappear as a vigorous force contributing anew to the development of Brazil.

Notes

Chapter 1: The Brazilian Concept of Nationalism

1. "A Psychologist Reflects on Brazil and the Brazilians," in Eric N. Baklanoff (ed.), *New Perspectives of Brazil* (Nashville, Tenn.: Vanderbilt University Press, 1966), p. 266.

2. Sérgio Buarque de Holanda, *Raízes do Brazil* (Rio de Janeiro: José Olympio, 1936), pp. 101, 143–44.

3. José Honório Rodrigues, *Aspirações Nacionais* (São Paulo: Editôra Fulgor, 1963), p. 42. Nicolão José Debané, author of *Nacionalismo Econômico*, also believed that "Brazilian nationality came into being before Brazil existed as a nation." (Quoted in Alvar Bomilcar, *A Política no Brasil ou o Nacionalismo Radical* [Rio de Janeiro: Leite Ribeiro e Maurillo Editores, 1921], p. 81.) See also Elysio de Carvalho, *Os Bastiões da Nacionalidade* (Rio de Janeiro: Annuário do Brasil, 1922), p. 13.

4. Barbosa Lima Sobrinho, *Desde Quando Somos Nacionalistas?* (Rio de Janeiro: Editôra Civilização Brasileira, 1963), p. 11.

5. Paulo Prado, *Retrato do Brasil* (6th ed.; Rio de Janeiro: José Olympio, 1962), p. 40.

6. There are numerous examples. For sixteenth-century Jesuit descriptions of Brazil, see *Cartas Jesuíticas II, Cartas Avulsas* (Rio de Janeiro: Oficina Industrial Gráfica, 1931). For a seventeenth-century defense of Brazil by a Portuguese immigrant, see Ambrósio Fernandes Brandão, *Diálogos das Grandezas do Brasil* (Rio de Janeiro: Academia Brasileira das Letras, 1930).

7. Lima Sobrinho, *op. cit.,* p. 12.

8. De Cavalho, *op. cit.,* pp. 26–27.

9. Hermes Lima, "Variações Críticas sôbre o Nacionalismo," *Revista Brasiliense,* No. 18 (July-August, 1958), p. 8.

10. Júlio Barbuda, *Literatura Brasileira* (Bahia: Estabelecimento dos Dois Mundos, 1916), pp. 57–58.

11. See Cândido Mendes de Almeida, *Nacionalismo e Desenvolvimento* (Rio de Janeiro: Instituto Brasileiro de Estudos Afro-Asiáticos, 1963); and Hélio Jaguaribe, *O Nacionalismo na Atualidade Brasileira* (Rio de Janeiro: Ministério da Educação, 1958).

12. Nelson Werneck Sodré, *Raízes Históricas do Nacionalismo Brasileiro* (Rio de Janeiro: Ministério da Educação, 1960), pp. 30–31.

Chapter 2: The Formation of Brazil and the Cult of Nativism

1. An abridged English version of the letter can be found in E. Bradford Burns (ed.), *A Documentary History of Brazil* (New York: Alfred A. Knopf, 1966), pp. 20–29.

2. *Cartas Jesuíticas II, Cartas Avulsas,* p. 150.

3. *Ibid.,* pp. 263–65.

4. These quotations are from Samuel Putnam, *Marvelous Journey: Four Centuries of Brazilian Literature* (New York: Alfred A. Knopf, 1948), pp. 57–58.

5. Frei Vicente do Salvador, *História do Brasil* (3d ed.; São Paulo: Melhoramentos, 1931), p. 153.

6. For a sampling of their opinions, see Rodrigues, *Aspirações Nacionais,* p. 43; Lima Sobrinho, *Desde Quando Somos Nacionalistas?,* pp. 16–17; Sílvio Romero, *História da Literatura Brasileira* (2d ed.; Rio de Janeiro: Garnier, 1902), I, 20. Foreign viewpoints seem to be much the same, for example, Arthur P. Whitaker, *Nationalism in Latin America* (Gainesville, Fla.: University of Florida Press, 1962), p. 26.

7. De Carvalho, *Os Bastiões da Nacionalidade,* p. 16.

8. João Capistrano de Abreu, *Capítulos da História Colonial* (4th ed.; Rio de Janeiro: Sociedade Capistrano de Abreu, 1944), p. 175.

9. Putnam, *op. cit.,* pp. 63–64.

10. "The predominant note in the author of the *History of Portuguese America* is patriotism; he loves this country; his book is a kind of patriotic hymn," wrote Sílvio Romero. (*História da Literatura Brasileira,* I, 170; see also pages 172–73.)

11. Sebastião da Rocha Pita, *História da América Portuguêsa* (Bahia: Imprensa Econômica, 1878), p. 3.

12. Both Putnam in *Marvelous Journey* (p. 86) and Manuel Bandeira in *A Brief History of Brazilian Literature* (Washington, D.C.: Brazilian-American Cultural Institute, 1964) (p. 56) regard *Caramurú* as precociously patriotic.

13. Quoted in the introduction by João de Barros to the prose edition of *O Caramurú* (Lisbon: Sá da Costa, 1958), p. 7.

14. Romero, *op. cit.,* I, 363.

15. Barbuda, *Literatura Brasileira,* p. 58. Most historians of Brazilian intellectual development concur. Antônio Cândido says that "literary activity is a part of the force constructing a free country," and that "literature . . . becomes the general language of a society in search of self-knowledge." (*Formação da Literatura Brasileira* [São Paulo: Livraria Martins Editôra, 1964], I, 28, 30.)

16. Jaguaribe, *O Nacionalismo na Atualidade Brasileira,* p. 21.

17. Cosío Villegas, "Nacionalismo e Desenvolvimento," *Revista Brasileira de Política Internacional* (Rio de Janeiro), V (December, 1962), 681. The Mexican Xavier Tavera Alfaro, writing on the creation of the feeling of nationality in eighteenth-century Mexico, affirms that Mexican periodicals of that time contained an "expression of Nationalist sentiment and consciousness." Furthermore, it was the writers who increased "the creole nationalist sentiment." (*El Nacionalismo en la Prensa Mexicana del Siglo XVIII* [Mexico City: Editorial Veracruz, 1963], pp. xxii, lxx.)

18. Víctor Andrés Belaúnde, *Bolívar and the Political Thought of the Spanish American Revolution* (Baltimore: Johns Hopkins University Press, 1938), pp. 118–19.

19. Quoted in R. A. Humphreys and John Lynch (eds.), *The Origins of the Latin American Revolutions* (New York: Alfred A. Knopf, 1965), p. 295.

20. João Rodrigues de Brito, *Cartas Econômico-Políticas* (Bahia: Imprensa Oficial do Estado, 1924), p. 28.

21. *Ibid.*, p. 85.

22. Quoted in Miguel Costa Filho, "A Formação da Nacionalidade Brasileira," *Revista do Instituto Histórico e Geográfico Brasileiro*, CCXXXVII (October–December, 1957), 134.

23. John Luccock, *Notes on Rio de Janeiro and the Southern Parts of Brazil* (London: Samuel Leigh, 1820), pp. 567–68.

24. *Ibid.*, p. 569.

25. In this context, Charles C. Griffin observed that "only in Brazil has Latin American nationalism escaped being a dividing force." ("An Essay on Regionalism and Nationalism in Latin American Historiography," *Journal of World History*, VIII [1964], p. 377.) Wilson Martins has also observed that Brazilian national sentiment has been a unifying force since early colonial days. ("Brazilian Politics," *Luso-Brazilian Review*, I [December, 1964], 33).

Chapter 3: *The Defensive Nationalism of the Nineteenth Century*

1. Quoted in Sérgio Corrêa de Costa, *Every Inch a King* (New York: Macmillan, 1953), pp. 166–67.

2. Quoted in Lima Sobrinho, *Desde Quando Somos Nacionalistas?*, p. 43.

3. Quoted, *ibid.*, p. 37.

4. See Carlos Pereyra, *El Pensamiento Político de Alberdi* (Madrid, n.d.), pp. 253–57.

5. Pedro de Córdoba, *La Coalición contra la Argentina*. The quotation is from the Portuguese-language edition, entitled *Alerta! . . . (Será Ameaça Vã?)* (Rio de Janeiro: Leite Ribeiro e Maurillo, 1917), p. 36.

6. Sargento Albuquerque, *A Cilada Argentina Contra o Brasil* (Rio de Janeiro: Monitor Mercantil, 1917), pp. 12–14.

7. Boyd C. Shafer discusses the role of foreign enemies in creating nationalist sentiment in his *Nationalism: Interpreters and Interpretations*, Publication No. 20 of the Service Center for Teachers of History (Washington, D.C.: American Historical Association, 1959), pp. 8–9. Similar views with regard to Latin America in general and Brazil in particular can be found in Lima Sobrinho, *op. cit.*, pp. 11–21; Roland Corbisier, *Formação e Problema da Cultura Brasileira* (Rio de Janeiro: Ministério da Educação, 1960), p. 60; and Cosío Villegas, "Nacionalismo e Desenvolvimento," pp. 685–86. Professor Cândido Mendes de Almeida, in an interview with the author in 1965, also stressed the importance of this point.

An external threat also helped to consolidate national feeling in the United States in the nineteenth century. Writing of the War of 1812, Albert Gallatin observed that "the war has renewed and reinstated the national feeling and character which the Revolution had given, and which were daily lessened. The people have now more general objectives of attachment. . . . They are more Americans; they feel and act more as a nation; and I hope that the permanency of the Union is thereby better secured." (*Writings of Albert Gallatin,* ed. Henry Adams [Philadelphia: J. B. Lippincott, 1879], I, 700.)

8. Lima Sobrinho, *op. cit.,* p. 11.

9. Quoted in José Honório Rodrigues, *Brazil and Africa* (Berkeley: University of California Press, 1966), p. 189.

10. Gilberto Amado, *História da Minha Infância* (Rio de Janeiro: José Olympio, 1954), p. 40.

11. Januário da Cunha Barbosa, "Discurso," *Revista do Instituto Histórico e Geográfico Brasileiro* (2d ed.), I, (1839), 12.

12. *Ibid.,* pp. 12–13.

13. *Ibid.,* p. 19.

14. Visconde de São Leopoldo, "Programma Histórico," *Revista do Instituto Histórico e Geográfico Brasileiro* (2d ed.), I (1839), 77–78.

15. Cunha Barbosa, *op. cit.,* p. 18.

16. Karl F. P. von Martius, "Como se Deve Escrever a História do Brasil," *Revista do Instituto Histórico e Geográfico Brasileiro,* VI (1844) 389–92. The English translation, "How the History of Brazil Should Be Written," appears in E. Bradford Burns (ed.), *Perspectives on Brazilian History* (New York: Columbia University Press, 1967), pp. 21–42.

17. *Ibid.,* p. 40. José Honório Rodrigues has also emphasized the role history can play in the promotion and development of nationalism: "To rectify our historical interpretations, official and academic, to put them at the service of the people and the nation, is the great project awaited by the younger generations. By doing so, we will make of history in this state of our evolution a legitimate instrument to defend our national interests and to emancipate our country. History thereby will serve our people and our fatherland." (José Honório Rodrigues, *História e Historiadores do Brasil* [São Paulo: Fulgor, 1965], p. 10.)

18. Quoted in Carlos Maul, *Nacionalismo e Comunismo* (Rio de Janeiro: Baptista da Souza, 1936), p. 183.

19. Quoted in Nelson Werneck Sodré, *História da Literatura Brasileira* (3d ed.; Rio de Janeiro: José Olympio, 1960), p. 255.

20. Francisco Adolfo de Varnhagen, *História Geral do Brasil* (1st ed.: Rio de Janeiro: Laemmert, 1854), I, 244.

21. Romero, *História da Literatura Brasileira,* I, 11.

22. *Ibid.,* p. 102.

23. João Capistrano de Abreu, "O Carácter Nacional e as Origens do Povo Brasileiro," *O Globo* (Rio de Janeiro), March 9, 1876, p. 3.

24. For a discussion of the role of the military in Brazilian history, see John J. Johnson, *The Military and Society in Latin America* (Stanford: Stanford University Press, 1964), pp. 193, 196–221; also Luiz Toledo Machado, *Conceito de Nacionalismo* (São Paulo: Editôra Fulgor, 1960), p. 194.

Chapter 4: The New Brazil and the Foundations of Twentieth-Century Nationalism

1. From the preface to Bomilcar, *A Política no Brasil ou o Nacionalismo Econômico,* p. v.

2. José Honório Rodrigues, "Capistrano de Abreu e a Historiografia Brasileira," *Revista do Instituto Histórico e Geográfico Brasileiro,* CCXXI (October-December, 1963). An English translation of this extremely important essay appears in Burns (ed.), *Perspectives on Brazilian History,* pp. 156–180.

3. See José Honório Rodrigues, "Afonso de Taunay e o Revisionismo Histórico," *Revista de História de América,* LI (June, 1961), p. 126.

4. Euclides da Cunha, *Rebellion in the Backlands,* trans. Samuel Putnam (Chicago: University of Chicago Press, 1944), p. 405.

5. *Ibid.,* pp. 464, 78.

6. *Ibid.,* p. 481.

7. Lima Barreto, *Triste Fim de Policarpo Quaresma* (Rio de Janeiro: Typ. Revista dos Tribunaes, 1915), pp. 13–16.

8. Carvalho, *Os Bastiões da Nacionalidade,* p. 27.

9. Ronald de Carvalho and Elysio de Carvalho, *Afirmações, Um Agape de Intelectuaes* (Rio de Janeiro: Monitor Mercantil, 1921), p. 34.

10. José Vasconcelos, "Discurso de Cuauhtémoc en el ofrecimiento que México hace al Brasil de una estatua de Cuauhtémoc" (1923), *Obras Completas* (Mexico: Libreros Mexicanos Unidos, 1958), II, pp. 851–52.

11. Joaquim Maria Machado de Assis, *Dom Casmurro* (Berkeley: University of California Press, 1966), p. 252.

12. Quoted in Afrânio Coutinho, *A Literatura no Brasil* (Rio de Janeiro: Livraria São José, 1959), III, Part I, 460.

13. Ronald de Carvalho, *Estudos Brasileiros* (1st series) (Rio de Janeiro: Anuário do Brasil, 1924), pp. 62–63.

14. Carlos Drummond de Andrade, "Explicação," *Alguma Poesia* (Belo Horizonte: Edições Pindorama, 1930). Cited by Rodrigues, *Aspirações Nacionais,* p. 155.

15. Quoted in Mário da Silva Brito, *História do Modernismo Brasileiro* (São Paulo: Edição Saraiva, 1958), p. 153.

16. Quoted in Afrânio Coutinho, *Conceito da Literatura Brasileira* (Rio de Janeiro: Livraria Acadêmica, 1960), p. 38.

17. Prado, *Retrato do Brasil* (6th ed.), pp. 3, 99, 101.

18. Quoted in Richard M. Morse (ed.), *The Bandeirantes* (New York: Alfred A. Knopf, 1965), p. 201.

19. Francisco de Assis Barbosa, *Achados do Vento* (Rio de Janeiro: Ministério da Educação, 1958), p. 13.

20. Bomilcar, *op. cit.,* p. 130.

21. Padre Antônio Carmelo, "Unamo-nos," *Brazilea,* I, No. 2 (February, 1917), 70–71.

22. Gilberto Freyre, *The Masters and the Slaves,* trans. Samuel Putnam (abridged ed.; New York: Alfred A. Knopf, 1964), p. 45.

23. See the study of Jackson de Figueiredo by Francisco Iglésias, "Estudo sôbre o Pensamento Reacionário: Jackson de Figueiredo," *Revista Brasileira de Ciências Sociais,* II (July, 1962), 3–52.

Chapter 5: *Getúlio Vargas and Economic Nationalism*

1. Letter dated January 28, 1907, from G. L. Lorillard to Secretary of State Elihu Root. National Archives of the United States, Brazilian Dispatches, CXIX, No. 101.

2. Getúlio Vargas, *A Nova Política do Brasil* (Rio de Janeiro: José Olympio, 1940), VI, 155.

3. *A Liga Americana* (Rio de Janeiro), No. 2 (November 7, 1839), p. 4.

4. Alberto Tôrres, *O Problema Nacional Brasileiro* (Rio de Janeiro: Imprensa Nacional, 1914), pp. 112, 115–16, 122.

5. *Ibid.*, p. 142.

6. See the essays of Luís Suárez, "The Crisis in Brazilian Society and Economy," and of Josué de Castro, "Colonialism, Hunger, and Progress," in Irving L. Horowitz, *Revolution in Brazil: Politics and Society in a Developing Nation* (New York: E. P. Dutton, 1964). (The inhibiting effect of the vestiges of colonial institutions on contemporary development is also the general theme of Nelson Werneck Sodré, *Raízes Históricas do Nacionalismo Brasileiro*.

7. General Pery Bevilacqua, in a speech in São Paulo, December 15, 1964; quoted in Euzébio Rocha, *Brasil País Ameaçado e o Acôrdo de Garantias* (São Paulo: Editôra Fulgor, 1965), p. 45.

8. Quoted in Affonso Henriques, *Ascensão e Queda de Getúlio Vargas* (Rio de Janeiro: Distribuidora Record, 1966), III, 207.

9. Olympio Guilherme, *O Nacionalismo e a Política Internacional do Brasil* (São Paulo: Editôra Fulgor, 1957), p. 60.

10. *The New York Times*, August 25, 1954, p. 2.

11. Nerêu Ramos, *Nacionalização do Ensino* (Florianópolis, Santa Catarina: Imprensa Oficial do Estado, 1938), pp. 7–8.

12. Quoted in Sérgio Macedo, *Getúlio Vargas e o Culto à Nacionalidade* (Rio de Janeiro: Gráfica Olímpica Miguel Couto, 1941), p. 15.

13. See John J. Johnson, *Political Change in Latin America: The Emergence of the Middle Sectors* (Stanford: Stanford University Press, 1958), p. 9. In another study, Johnson refers to the period prior to 1930 as one of "aristocratic nationalism . . . fashioned by the intellectuals"; the period after 1930 he calls a "populist one." ("The New Latin American Nationalism," *Yale Review*, Winter, 1965, pp. 188, 191.)

14. Vargas, *op. cit.*, V, 124.

15. The full text of Vargas' suicide note will be found in *The New York Times*, August 25, 1954, p. 2. Reproduced in Burns (ed.), *A Documentary History of Brazil*, pp. 368–371.

Chapter 6: Action and Reaction

1. Pimentel Gomes, *O Brasil entre as Cinco Maiores Potências no Fim dêste Século* (Rio de Janeiro: Editôra Leitura, 1964), p. 9.

2. Eduardo Prado, *A Ilusão Americana* (3d ed.; São Paulo: Editôra Brasiliense, 1961), pp. 111, 97.

3. Mendes de Almeida, *Nacionalismo e Desenvolvimento;* Souza Barros, *Subdesenvolvimento: Nordeste e Nacionalismo* (São Paulo: Editôra Fulgor, 1964), p. 116. Professor Albert O. Hirschman has analyzed the relationship between nationalism and development: "The aim of economic development is far more than an increase in per capita income: it is also, and more importantly, this 'conquest of decision centers,' which were previously in foreign hands, and a new ability to strike out on one's own, economically, po-

litically, and intellectually. For this reason, the quest for development is also a quest for self-discovery and self-affirmation and thus comes to be indissolubly tied to a new nationalism which is so noticeable a feature of the intellectual scene in Latin America." (*Latin American Issues* [New York: The Twentieth Century Fund, 1961], p. 35.)

4. Juscelino Kubitschek, *A Marcha do Amanhecer* (São Paulo: Bestseller, 1962), p. 114.

5. Adacir Soares and Vito Diniz Neto, "60 Dias nas Selvas," *Manchete* (Rio de Janeiro), July 10, 1965, p. 66.

6. See José Honório Rodrigues, *Interêsse Nacional e Política Externa* (Rio de Janeiro: Civilização Brasileira, 1966), p. 176.

7. San Tiago Dantas, *Política Externa Independente* (Rio de Janeiro: Civilização Brasileira, 1962), pp. 5, 17–18.

8. Quoted in Horowitz, *Revolution in Brazil*, p. 42.

9. *Palavra de Arraes. Textos de Miguel Arraes* (Rio de Janeiro: Editôra Civilização Brasileira, 1966), pp. 52–53, 55.

10. Dantas, *op. cit.*, p. 5.

11. The results of the poll were published in Lloyd A. Free, *Some International Implications of the Political Psychology of Brazilians* (Princeton: The Institute for International Social Research, 1961); see pp. 35, 37, 24. José Honório Rodrigues accepts the findings of the poll. (*Aspirações Nacionais*, p. 22.)

12. *Newsweek*, November 14, 1966, p. 56. There were other reports in the U.S. press that the United States had used its influence to bring about the fall of Goulart; see, for example, Sidney Lens, "Brazil's Police State," *The Progressive*, December, 1966, p. 33. Lens wrote in part: "In Brazil, the United States was on the scene with its navy and was prepared to send in millions in armaments to any state government that would raise the flag of insurgency against the national government. It was ready, in other words, to foment a civil war." Professor Thomas E. Skidmore considered the question of United States involvement in his study *Politics in Brazil, 1930–1964: An Experiment in Democracy* (New York: Oxford University Press, 1967), Appendix: "The United States Role in João Goulart's Fall." He suggests there (p. 324) as well as in the text itself (pp. 270–71) that the United States refused financial aid to Goulart in the hope that increasing financial pressure on his administration might help to accelerate his overthrow.

13. *Brazil Herald* (Rio de Janeiro), December 3, 1966, p. 3.

14. Quoted in José de Bálsamo, *Jânio e a Petrobrás* (São Paulo: Fulgor, 1960), p. 63.

15. *Ibid.*, p. 60.

16. *Manchete* (Rio de Janeiro), July 10, 1965, p. 98.

17. Mário Afonso Carneiro, "Opinião Militar," *Cadernos Brasileiros*, No. 38 (November-December, 1966), p. 28.

18. Quoted in Rocha, *Brasil País Ameaçado e o Acôrdo de Garantias*, p. 45.

19. "Brasil Pergunta," *Realidade*, No. 3 (June, 1966), p. 122.

20. From a speech made in Belém, reported in the *Brazil Herald* (Rio de Janeiro), June 14, 1965, p. 13.

21. From a speech made in Manaus, reported in the *Jornal do Brasil* (Rio de Janeiro), December 5, 1966, pp. 1, 22. See also Castelo Branco's

speech in Belém, reported in the *Correio da Manhã* (Rio de Janeiro), September 6, 1964, p. 12.

22. Gustavo Corção, *Patriotismo e Nacionalismo* (Rio de Janeiro: Editôra Presença [1963?]), pp. 8, 49.

23. See Assis Chateaubriand, "O Nosso Reino Não é o Dêste Mundo Indú-Arabe," *O Jornal* (Rio de Janeiro), February 2, 1961, p. 3. The equation was made many decades before the issue was raised in the popular mind. A highly respected Brazilian writer, José Maria dos Santos, in his *A Política Geral do Brasil* (São Paulo: J. Magalhães, 1930), condemned both Communism and nationalism because both "led to simple despotism" (p. 534). The equation continues until today. In a statement made in early February, 1968, Manoel Nascimento Brito, director of the *Jornal do Brasil,* warned his readers to "avoid Communist propaganda which is often cloaked in the guise of nationalism." (*The Times of the Americas,* February 14, 1968, p. 4.)

24. See Rocha, *Brasil País Ameaçado e o Acôrdo de Garantias,* p. 46.

25. Maul, *Nacionalismo e Comunismo,* p. 13.

26. Quoted by Carneiro, *op. cit.,* p. 25. An excellent sampling of nationalist opposition to the Dominican intervention can be found in *Política Externa Independente,* No. 2 (August, 1965).

27. Carlos Lacerda, "Natureza, Crise e Rumos da Revolução," *O Estado de São Paulo,* April 3, 1966, p. 159.

28. Editorial in *Tribuna da Imprensa* (Rio de Janeiro), November 11, 1966, p. 1.

29. "Questionário Proposto pela Revista Civilização Brasileira a Personalidades da Vida Pública Nacional," *Revista Civilização Brasileira,* No. 7 (May, 1966), pp. 54–55.

30. Interview with Henrique Teixeira Lott, in *Revista Civilização Brasileira,* No. 1 (May, 1965), p. 4.

31. "Questionário Proposto . . . ," pp. 51, 71.

32. "Brasil Pergunta," p. 122.

33. "Questionário Proposto . . . ," pp. 46–47.

34. *Ultima Hora* (Rio de Janeiro), February 23, 1967, p. 1.

35. *Correio da Manhã* (Rio de Janeiro), January 29, 1967, p. 6; February 14, 1967, p. 8.

36. *O Globo* (Rio de Janeiro), June 4, 1967, p. 11.

37. Hermano Alves, "Força Interamericana Permanente de Paz: O Braço Armado do Império," *Política Externa Independente,* No. 2 (August, 1965), p. 142.

38. *The Times of the Americas,* January 10, 1968, p. 1.

Chapter 7: The Reckoning

1. Arnold Toynbee, *Between Maule and Amazon* (New York: Oxford University Press, 1967), p. 148.

Bibliographical Essay

For much of the bibliographical data on the general conception of nationalism, I refer the reader to Boyd C. Shafer, *Nationalism: Interpreters and Interpretations,* Publication No. 20 of the Service Center for Teachers of History of the American Historical Association (Washington, D.C., 1959). A number of works on nationalism have been published since 1959, of which Carleton J. H. Hayes' *Nationalism: A Religion* (New York: Macmillan, 1960), Leonard W. Doob's *Patriotism and Nationalism: Their Psychological Foundations* (New Haven: Yale University Press, 1964), and Louis J. Snyder's *The Dynamics of Nationalism* (Princeton: Van Nostrand, 1964) are representative.

The pioneer study of Latin American nationalism in English is Arthur P. Whitaker's volume of essays entitled *Nationalism in Latin America: Past and Present* (Gainesville: University of Florida Press, 1962). Kalman H. Silvert (ed.), *Expectant Peoples: Nationalism and Development* (New York: Random House, 1963), contains a number of essays on Latin American countries, including Frank Bonilla's "A National Ideology for Development: Brazil." Two recent books on the historical development of Latin American nationalism are Arthur P. Whitaker and David Jordan, *Nationalism in Contemporary Latin America* (New York: The Free Press, 1966) and Gerhard Masur, *Nationalism in Latin America: Diversity and Unity* (New York: Macmillan, 1966). Each book devotes a brief chapter to Brazilian nationalism, and the Whitaker-Jordan book contains a bibliographical guide.

A number of articles on Latin American nationalism have also appeared, among the best of which are Robert J. Alexander, "Nationalism, Latin America's Predominant Ideology," *Journal of International Affairs,* Fall, 1961; Kalman H. Silvert, "Nationalism in Latin America," *The Annals of the American Academy of Political and Social Science,* March, 1961; Charles C. Griffin, "An Essay on Regionalism and Nationalism in Latin American Historiography," *Journal of World History* (1962); John J. Johnson, "The New Latin American Nationalism," *Yale Review*, December, 1964; and Arthur P. Whitaker, "Nationalism and Social Change in Latin America," in Joseph Maier and Richard W. Weatherhead (eds.), *The Politics of Change in Latin America* (New York: Frederick A. Praeger, 1964). Among the excellent monographic studies on specific aspects of Latin American nationalism, Ernest Halperin, *Nationalism and Communism in Chile* (Cambridge, Mass.: M.I.T. Press, 1965), Samuel L. Baily, *Labor, Nationalism and Politics in Argentina* (New Brunswick: Rutgers University Press, 1967), and Frederick C. Turner, *The Dynamic of Mexican Nationalism* (Chapel Hill: University of Carolina Press, 1968) are to be recommended.

The present essay on the growth of Brazilian nationalism obviously fits within the broader scope of Brazilian historical evolution. For the reader who may wish to delve more deeply into Brazil's past, there is, unfortunately, no satisfactory interpretative one-volume history of Brazil in any language. For the present, the reader may consult the expository *A History of Brazil*, by João Pandiá Calógeras (Chapel Hill: University of North Carolina Press, 1939), and the more detailed *A History of Modern Brazil, 1889–1964*, by José Mária Bello (Stanford: Stanford University Press, 1964), with a concluding chapter by Rollie E. Poppino. An examination of Brazilian historians and their writings will be found in E. Bradford Burns (ed.), *Perspectives on Brazilian History* (New York: Columbia University Press, 1967). The views of José Honório Rodrigues, Brazil's leading authority on national historiography, appear in two informative volumes, *História e Historiadores do Brasil* (São Paulo: Editôra Fulgor, 1965) and *Vida e História* (Rio de Janeiro: Civilização Brasileira, 1966).

Two perceptive interpretive studies of Brazil, Charles Wagley's *An Introduction to Brazil* (New York: Columbia University Press, 1963) and Rollie E. Poppino's *Brazil: The Land and People* (New York: Oxford University Press, 1968), are strongly recommended. Wagley's engaging concluding chapter, "If I Were a Brazilian," is an excellent statement of Brazilian feelings on nationalism. Both works also contain good bibliographies. William Lytle Shurz presents a more personal approach in his *Brazil: The Infinite Country* (New York: E. P. Dutton, 1961). Two collections of essays by well-known Brazilianists merit attention: Lawrence F. Hill (ed.), *Brazil* (Berkeley: University of California Press, 1947), and T. Lynn Smith and Alexander Marchant (eds.), *Brazil: Portrait of Half a Continent* (New York: Dryden, 1951).

Obviously of fundamental importance is the Brazilian's interpretation of his own country. A number of these studies have been translated into English. Gilberto Freyre's *The Masters and the Slaves,* an analysis of the amalgamation of three races and the emergence of a "Brazilian civilization," has been published in several editions, including one in paperback (New York: Alfred A. Knopf, 1964). Also highly recommended is this eminent scholar's interpretative *New World in the Tropics* (New York: Alfred A. Knopf, 1959). Clodomir Vianna Moog has written a controversial interpretation, *Bandeirantes and Pioneers* (New York: George Braziller, 1964), in which he compares and contrasts the history of Brazil and of the United States. Manoel de Oliveira Lima's *The Evolution of Brazil Compared with that of Spanish and Anglo-Saxon America* (New York: Russell and Russell, 1966) is another comparative study, one that places Brazilian history in its hemispheric context. Two brief and insightful Portuguese-language studies of Brazil and the Brazilian are Paulo Prado's *Retrato do Brasil* (São Paulo, 1928), and Sérgio Buarque de Holanda's *Raízes do Brasil* (Rio de Janeiro: José Olympio, 1936).

Much can be learned about Brazil through reading the novels and short stories of the country's foremost literary figure, Machado de Assis. Many of his works have been translated into English, among them *Dom Casmurro* (New York: Noonday Press, 1953), *Epitaph of a Small Winner* (New York: Noonday Press, 1956), and *Essau and Jacob* (Berkeley: University of California Press, 1965).

The most important study of the background of Brazilian nationalism is Barbosa Lima Sobrinho's *Desde Quando Somos Nacionalistas?* (Rio de Janeiro: Editôra Civilização Brasileira, 1963). The author does not consider his short work a history of nationalism but rather "a recapitulation of various manifestations of Brazilian nationalism." Regarding nationalism as the result of foreign threats, he traces Brazil's reactions to challenges from the Dutch, Portuguese, British, Germans, Japanese, and North Americans. The book abounds with factual information and suggests many topics future scholars can explore. A second useful historical approach to Brazilian nationalism can be found in Nelson Werneck Sodré's *Raízes Históricas do Nacionalismo Brasileiro* (Rio de Janeiro: Ministério de Educação, 1960). Although adhering perhaps too closely to a Marxian interpretation, the essay is well done and thought-provoking. Sodré traces through Brazilian history the constantly expanding support given to nationalism as a force capable of redeeming Brazil. He sees nationalism as the "liberator," that is, the force that will destroy the colonial past and project Brazil into the future. José Honório Rodrigues also contributes to the historical study of nationalism with his admirable *Aspiraçoes Nacionais* (São Paulo: Fulgor, 1963), recently translated into English as *The Brazilians: Their Character and Aspirations* (Austin: University of Texas Press, 1967).

Most of the literature on the three periods of Brazilian nationalism discussed in the present study may be found in works dealing with a wide variety of subjects. There is no study of colonial nativism as such; the best treatment of the subject will be found in the literary histories. In his *Pequena História da Literatura Brasileira* (Rio de Janeiro: Briguiet, 1919), Ronald de Carvalho devotes a chapter to "The Seventeenth Century: The Dawn of Nativist Sentiment." Manoel de Oliveira Lima studies the nativistic writers in his *Aspectos da Littera-tura Colonial Brasileira* (Leipzig: Brockhaus, 1896). Excellent editions have appeared in Portuguese of most of the nativistic writers mentioned in Chapter 2 of this book. Those interested in the movement will want to read the chroniclers Ambrósio Fernandes Brandão and André João Antonil, the historian Sebastião da Rocha Pita, and the poets José Basílio da Gama and José de Santa Rita Durão. The idea of Brazil as a terrestrial paradise appears frequently in nativistic literature. The concept receives careful examination in Sérgio Buarque de Holanda's masterful *Visão do Paraíso* (Rio de Janeiro: José Olympio, 1959) and is more briefly discussed in E. Bradford Burns, "The Brazilian Jesuit Letters, a Sixteenth Century View of Portuguese America," *Revista da Faculdade de Ciências* (Coimbra), XXXIX (1967) and in Henri Baudet, *Paradise on Earth: Some Thoughts on European Images of Non-European Man* (New Haven: Yale University Press, 1965). A general cultural history that peripherally discusses the growth of nativism is Fernando de Azevedo's voluminous *Brazilian Culture: An Introduction to the Study of Culture in Brazil* (New York: Macmillan, 1950). A. K. Manchester describes the emergence of a native elite in "The Rise of the Brazilian Aristocracy," *Hispanic American Historical Review*, XI (1931). João Capistrano de Abreu concentrates on the formation of Brazilian "types" and the change of Brazilian psychology during the colonial period in *Capítulos de História Colonial* (Rio de Janeiro: Sociedade Capistrano de Abreu, 1928). The majority of Manoel de Oliveira Lima's *Formação Histórica da Nacionalidade Brasileira* (Rio de Janeiro: Editôra Leitura, 1944) is devoted to the growth of nativist sentiment during the colonial period.

Much of the information on the patterns of nineteenth-century nationalism is also to be found in the literary histories. The best general discussions of cultural nationalism in that century appear in the works of Sílvio Romero, particularly in his two-volume *História da Literatura Brasileira* (2d ed.; Rio de Janeiro: Garnier, 1902–03). Pedro Júlio

Barbuda's *Literatura Brasileira* (Bahia: Estabelecimento dos Dois Mundos, 1916), a general discussion of the emergence of Brazil and of the background of a national literature, also concerns itself with the formation of the Brazilian soul and with the basis for Brazilian nationality. Two works in English trace the development of cultural nationalism: Samuel Putnam's *Marvelous Journey: Four Centuries of Brazilian Literature* (New York: Alfred A. Knopf, 1948) and Manuel Bandeira's *A Brief History of Brazilian Literature* (Washington, D.C.: Brazilian-American Cultural Institute, 1964). Nelson Werneck Sodré's *História da Literatura Brasileira* (3d ed.; Rio de Janeiro: José Olympio, 1960) contains an excellent discussion of the history of Indianism in Brazil and its relation to both nativism and nationalism. One should also consult *The Indian in Brazilian Literature,* by David Miller Driver (New York: The Hispanic Institute, 1942). For an idea of how intellectuals have viewed the Negro in Brazilian society, the reader may consult the excellent study of Raymond S. Sayers, *The Negro in Brazilian Literature* (New York: The Hispanic Institute, 1956). A suggestive intellectual history, concentrating on the nineteenth century, is João Cruz Costa's *A History of Ideas in Brazil: The Development of Philosophy in Brazil and the Evolution of Natural History* (Berkeley: University of California Press, 1964). The pages of the *Revista do Instituto Histórico e Geográfico Brasileiro,* which began publication in 1839, provide many insights into the development of nationalism: the interest in the Indian, the suspicion of foreign scholars, the praise of Brazil and its natural beauty, the glorification of national heroes, and so forth.

No work better gives the flavor of nationalism at the turn of the century than Afonso Celso's *Porque Me Ufano do Meu País,* which was first published in 1901 and is now in its fourteenth edition. The intense cultural nationalism of the early twentieth century lives in the pages of Mário da Silva Brito's *História do Modernismo Brasileiro. Antecedentes da Semana de Arte Moderna* (São Paulo: Saraiva, 1958). The drama of Modern Art Week and its contributions to nationalism are the subject of a long essay by Mário da Silva Brito in *A Literatura no Brasil,* Vol. III, Part I, ed. by Afrânio Coutinho (Rio de Janeiro: Livraria São José, 1959). For an account in English of the significance of the Modern Art Week to the development of Brazilian cultural nationalism, see John Nist, *The Modernist Movement in Brazil* (Austin: University of Texas Press, 1967); his emphasis is on the contributions of the poets. Finally, Francisco de Assis Barbosa has contributed an important essay on "Nacionalismo e Literatura" in his *Achados do Vento* (Rio de Janeiro: Ministério da Educação, 1958).

A number of studies on nationalism were published in the 1920's. In his *A Política no Brazil ou o Nacionalismo Radical* (Rio de Janeiro: Leite Ribeiro, 1921), Alvaro Bomilcar reviews the contemporary literature published on that topic and also gives considerable information on nationalist movements of the period. An excellent example of the nationalist writings of the 1920's is Elysio de Carvalho's *Os Bastiões da Nacionalidade* (Rio de Janeiro: Anuário do Brasil, 1922); the chapters "Origem do Sentimento Nacional Brasileiro," "Nacionalismo e Patriotismo," and "Nacionalismo Brasileiro" particularly capture the surging nationalistic spirit of the intellectuals of the period. Of similar interest are two essays of Ronald de Carvalho, "Bases da Nacionalidade Brasileira" and "A Psyche Brasileira," which appeared in *Estudos Brasileiros, 1ª Serie* (Rio de Janeiro: Anuário do Brasil, 1924). The first is an interpretive study of Brazilian history, the second a study of the formation of the national character.

The centennial celebrations of independence in 1922 gave birth to a plethora of patriotic literature, much of it ephemeral. Representative of the genre are Mecenas Rocha's *Problemas Nacionaes* (Belém: Livraria Bittencourt, 1922) and Eylsio de Carvalho's *A Realidade Brasileira* (Rio de Janeiro: Monitor Mercantil, 1922), both of which declared their faith in nationalism.

The background of economic nationalism is discussed in a commendable study by Nícia Vilela Luz, *A Luta pela Industrialização do Brasil* (São Paulo: Difusão Européia do Livro, 1961), which outlines the development of economic nationalism up to 1930. Alberto Tôrres, a major precursor of modern economic nationalism, wrote two works that merit study: *A Organização Nacional* (Rio de Janeiro: Imprensa Nacional, 1914) and *O Problema Nacional Brasileiro* (Rio de Janeiro: Imprensa Nacional, 1914). Heitor Ferreira Lima relates the careers of two outstanding advocates of industrialization, the Visconde de Mauá of the nineteenth century and Roberto Simonsen of the twentieth, in his *Mauá e Roberto Simonsen: Dois Pioneiros do Desenvolvimento* (São Paulo: Editôra Edaglet, 1963). Simonsen's own arguments favoring industrialization are put forth in *A Indústria em face da Economia Nacional* (São Paulo: Emprêsa Gráfica da Revista dos Tribunaes, 1937).

For an understanding of economic nationalism after 1930, it is best to go directly to the man who directed it, Getúlio Vargas. His ideas and statements will be found in *A Nova Política do Brasil* (10 vols.; Rio de Janeiro: José Olympio, 1938–45). Vargas' statements on the petroleum industry have been collected in *A Política Nacionalista do Petróleo no Brasil* (Rio de Janeiro: Tempo Brasileiro, 1964).

The ideological basis of present-day "developmental nationalism" is presented in three penetrating analyses of modern Brazilian nationalism. The first is Hélio Jaguaribe's *O Nacionalismo na Atualidade Brasileira* (Rio de Janeiro: Ministério da Educação, 1958). Jaguaribe's general discussion of nationalism in Brazil is followed by a detailed study of its relation to the issues of petroleum extraction, foreign capital, and foreign policy. Most of the ideas presented in this book are repeated in a shorter work published in Spanish, *Burguesia y Proletariado en el Nacionalismo Brasileiro* (Buenos Aires: Coyocán, 1961). A summary of his views in English appears in his article "The Dynamic of Brazilian Nationalism," in Claudio Véliz (ed.), *Obstacles to Change in Latin America* (New York: Oxford University Press, 1965). The second analysis is Hermes Lima's article "Variações Críticas sôbre o Nacionalismo," *Revista Brasiliense*, No. 18 (July-August, 1958). Lima discusses political and economic nationalism and the inextricable intertwining of the two. Cândido Mendes de Almeida is the author of the third of the analyses, *Nacionalismo e Desenvolvimento* (Rio de Janeiro: Instituto Brasileiro de Estudos Afro-Asiáticos, 1963), recently published in English as *Brazilian Nationalism and Development* (New York: Columbia University Press, 1968). Almeida ably details the connection between nationalism and development and the inter-action of the two.

For additional information on the vital concept of "developmental nationalism," the reader should consult Roland Corbisier, *Formação e Problema da Cultura Brasileira* (Rio de Janeiro: Ministério da Educação, 1960) and Álvaro Vieira Pinto, *Conciência e Realidade Nacional* (2 vols.; Rio de Janeiro: Ministério da Educação, 1960). Alexander Marchant has written a general essay, "Industrialism, Nationalism, and the People of Brazil," *Journal of International Affairs*, No. 92 (May, 1955) which presents industrialization and nationalism as complementary forces in contemporary Brazil.

Two informative articles in English treat the Instituto Superior de Estudos Brasileiros (ISEB) and its ideology of "developmental nationalism." The first is Frank Bonilla's "A National Ideology for Development: Brazil," in Kalman H. Silvert (ed.), *Expectant Peoples: Nationalism and Development* (New York: Random House, 1963). The second is Hermínio Martins' "Ideology and Development: 'Developmental Nationalism' in Brazil," in Paul Halmos (ed.), *Latin American Sociological Studies* (The Sociological Review Monograph No. 11) (Keele: Keele University Press, 1967).

To place contemporary economic nationalism in its proper perspective, I suggest two books by Celso Furtado: *The Economic Growth of Brasil: A Survey from Colonial to Modern Times* (Berkeley: University of California Press, 1963) and *Diagnosis of the Brazilian Crisis* (Berkeley: University of California Press, 1965). The necessity for land reform in Brazil is discussed in T. Lynn Smith's *Agrarian Reform in Latin America* (New York: Alfred A. Knopf, 1965).

Many of the seminal ideas of contemporary nationalism were first presented in articles that appeared in *Cadernos do Nosso Tempo,* a journal published irregularly in Rio de Janeiro between 1953 and 1956. The *Revista Brasiliense,* published in São Paulo in the years 1955–64, also regularly featured articles on Brazilian nationalism. Indicative of the wealth of material to be found in its issues would be: Heitor Ferreira Lima, "Capitais Nacionais e Investimentos Estrangeiros," No. 1 (September-October, 1955); Caio Prado Junior, "Nacionalismo Brasileiro e Capitais Estangeiros," No. 2 (November-December, 1955); Paulo Aves Pinto, "Aspectos da Penetração Imperialista no Brasil," No. 5 (May-June, 1956); Elias Chaves Neto, "Política de Neutralidade," No. 10 (March-April, 1957); Evaldo Martins, "Algumas Observações sôbre a Luta pela Emancipação Nacional," No. 11 (May-June, 1957); Octávio Ianni, "Aspectos do Nacionalismo Brasileiro," No. 14 (November-December, 1957); and Afrânio Coutinho, "A Literatura Brasileira e a Idéia Nacional," No. 17 (May-June, 1958).

The political history of Brazil between the Revolutions of 1930 and of 1964 is fully outlined in Thomas E. Skidmore's *Politics in Brazil, 1930–1964: An Experiment in Democracy* (New York: Oxford University Press, 1967). The text includes scattered discussions of the development and influence of contemporary nationalism. Two other recently published works dealing with more or less the same period, and which touch on the subject of nationalism, are Jordan M. Young's *The Brazilian Revolution of 1930 and the Aftermath* (New Brunswick: Rutgers University Press, 1967), and John W. F. Dulles' *Vargas of Brazil* (Austin: University of Texas Press, 1967).

The subject of an independent foreign policy for Brazil has received increasing attention. One of its most prolific and penetrating students is José Honório Rodrigues. In English, Rodrigues has published a general introduction to Brazilian diplomatic history, "The Foundations of Brazil's Foreign Policy," *International Affairs* (London), XXXVIII (July, 1962), and a plea for closer relations with Africa, *Africa and Brazil* (Berkeley: University of California Press, 1965). His *Interêsse Nacional e Política Externa* (Rio de Janeiro: Editôra Civilização Brasileira, 1966), states the nationalist point of view in foreign affairs. Jânio Quadros's views on an independent foreign policy for Brazil are set forth in his "Brazil's New Foreign Policy," *Foreign Affairs,* October, 1961. The principal speeches and writings of former Foreign Minister San Tiago Dantas can be found in his *Política Externa Independente* (Rio de Janeiro: Editôra Civilização Brasileira, 1962). For a short time, the nationalists published their own journal on foreign affairs, *Política Externa Independente.* The first issue (May, 1965) set forth the nationalist position on foreign relations and discussed the crisis of Pan Americanism. The second issue (August, 1965) was concerned primarily with the U.S. intervention in the Dominican Republic. The final issue (January, 1966) covered the inter-American system after the Dominican invasion and Brazil's relations with Africa. The fluctuations in Brazilian foreign policy from the ministry of the Baron of Rio-Branco to the present are traced in E. Bradford Burns, "Tradition and Variation in Brazilian Foreign Policy," *Journal of Inter-American Studies,* April, 1967.

In the past decade, there has been an avalanche of books on various aspects of nationalism published in Brazil. These books should be read with a good deal of caution. Highly emotional and anti-Yankee in tone, they represent the strongest current of contemporary nationalism, the left. They merit attention not for their objectivity (which is lacking) or their literary style (which is non-existent), but because they present the arguments, points of view, and rationale most frequently encountered among Brazilian nationalists. The following are only a few of such books but they are representative of their genre: Dagoberto Costa (of the Movimento Nacionalista Brasileiro) *et al., Sopram os Ventos da Liberdade. Antologia Nacionalista* (São Paulo: Fulgor, 1959); Souza Barros, *Subdesenvolvimento: Nordeste e Nacionalismo* (São Paulo: Fulgor, 1964); Olympio Guilherme, *O Nacionalismo e a Política Internacional do Brasil* (São Paulo: Fulgor, 1957); Gabriel de Rezende Passos, *Temas Nacionalistas* (São Paulo: Fulgor, 1961); Osny Duarte Perreira, *Estudos Nacionalistas* (Rio de Janeiro: Conquista, 1962); Luiz Toledo Machado, *Conceito de Nacionalismo* (São Paulo: Fulgor, 1960); Aguinaldo N. Marques, *Fundamentos do Nacionalismo* (São Paulo: Fulgor, 1960) Euzébio Rocha, *Brasil País Ameaçado e o Acôrdo de Garantias* (São Paulo: Fulgor, 1965); and Sérgio Magalhães, *Problema do Desenvolvimento Económico* (Rio de Janeiro: Editôra Civilização Brasileira, 1960). Their economic arguments have been summarized by Andrew Gunder Frank in his article "On the Mechanisms of Imperialism: The Case of Brazil," *Monthly Review,* September, 1964.

The *Revista Civilização Brasileira,* published more or less bimonthly in Rio de Janeiro since March, 1965, is the contemporary disseminator of nationalist thought. The magazine refers to itself as "the means by which studies and research about the national reality can be divulged." It too reflects a preference for the left and antagonism toward the United States. Its well-known contributors include Barbosa Lima Sobrinho, Nelson Werneck Sodré, Otto Mária Carpeaux, Dias Gomes, and Roland Corbisier, whose contributions ensure a high intellectual content for the *Revista.* The issues of the review contain a wealth of essays, articles, and reviews on national politics, international affairs, economics, and the arts; its pages reveal that nationalist thought remains unchanged after April 1, 1964.

The role of the military in modern Brazilian politics has been decisive. Both Edwin Lieuwen's *Arms and Politics in Latin America* (New York: Frederick A. Praeger, 1961) and John J. Johnson's *The Military and Society in Latin America* (Stanford: Stanford University Press, 1966) include discussions of the military in Brazil. Nelson Werneck Sodré provides a history of the Brazilian military establishment in his huge and factual *História Militar do Brasil* (Rio de Janeiro: Civilização Brasileira, 1965). The issue of *Cadernos Brasileiros,* No. 38 (November-December, 1966) entitled "Os Militares," contains excellent informative and analytic essays on various activities and attitudes of the military.

Finally, to give some balance, I recommend two books by conservative nationalists and one by a critic of nationalism. Jackson de Figueiredo stands out as the foremost advocate of a conservative nationalism based on the Portuguese, Roman Catholic past. His principal work on this subject was *Do Nacionalismo na Hora Presente* (Rio de Janeiro: Livraria Católica, 1921). Francisco Iglésias has made a superb study of Figueiredo's thought, "Estudo sôbre o Pensamento Reacionário: Jackson de Figueiredo," *Revista Brasileira de Ciências Sociais* (Belo Horizonte), II, No. 2 (July, 1962).

The most important rightist nationalist movement was Integralism in the 1930's. There is considerable literature about the Integralists, although little of it is objective. The principal statements of the movement's leader, Plínio Salgado, are found in *O Integralismo perante a Nação* (3d ed.; Rio de Janeiro: Livraria Clássica Brasileira, 1955). One of the strongest antinationalist statements of recent times is Gustavo Corção's *Patriotismo e Nacionalismo* (Rio de Janeiro: Editôra Presença, 1963[?]), a book that is the antithesis of the contemporary nationalistic literature so popular in Brazil.

Index

Abreu, João Capistrano de, 16, 46, 55
Academy of the Forgotten (Academia dos Esquecidos), 20–21
Africa, 6, 44, 96, 98
Afro-Asian Institute, 96
Alberdi, Juan Bautista, 36
Alencar, José de, 45
Algeria, 98
Alliance for Progress, 108
Almeida, Cândido Mendes de, 11, 101, 103, 128–29
Almeida, Guilherme de, 61
Almeida, Manoel Antônio de, 43
Alves, Francisco de Paula Rodrigues, 72
Alves Branco Tariff, 35
Amado, Gilberto, 38
Amado, Jorge, 65, 112
Amazon river, 5, 15, 86
American and Foreign Power Company, 100
Américo, Pedro, 46
Andrade, Carlos Drummond de, 62
Andrade, Doutel de, 123–24
Andrade, Mário de, 64, 67
Andrade, Oswald de, 67
Anta, 66
Antonil, André João, 20
Antropofagia, 66
Aranha, José Pereira da Graça, 54, 61, 63
Argentina, 36–37, 52, 123
Armitage, John, 41

Arraes, Miguel, 108, 109
Assis, Machado de, 54, 62, 63, 112
Associação Industrial, 79–80
Azevedo, Aluízio de, 6–7

Bahia, 15, 19, 20, 39
Bahia, Luís Alberto, 110
Bahia de Todos os Santos, 14
Barbosa, Francisco de Assis, 67
Barbosa, Januário da Cunha, 40, 41
Barbuda, Júlio, 9–10, 24
Barreto, Lima, 54, 58–60
Barros, Prudente de Moraes, 72
Barroso, Gustavo, 63–64, 66, 76
Basadre, Jorge, 24
Belaúnde, Víctor Andrés, 24
Belo Horizonte, 52
Bernardes, Arthur, 81
Bernhardt, Sarah, 53
Bevilacqua, General Pery, 118, 120
Bilac, Olavo, 54
Boiteux, Admiral Norton D., 119, 124–25
Bolívar, Simón, 31
Bolivia, 53, 107
Branco, Marshal Humberto Castelo, 114, 116, 119–20, 121 ff., 125–26
Brandâo, Ambrósio Fernandes, 13–14
Brasília, 93, 97, 111
Brazilian Academy of Letters, 61, 63
Brazilian Geographical and Historical Institute (Instituto Histórico e Geográfico Brasileiro), 110

Brazilian Institute of Economics, Sociology, and Politics (Instituto Brasileiro de Economia, Sociologia e Política), 102
Brazilian Labor Party (Partido Trabalhista Brasileiro), 87, 109, 131
Brito, João Rodrigues de, 25–26
Brizzola, Leonel, 99–100, 110
Bryan, William Jennings, 53
Bryce, James, 53
Bueno, Maria, 111

Cabral, Pedro Alvares, 12
Camarão, Felipe, 15
Caminha, Pero Vaz de, 12
Camões, Luís de, 5
Campos, Francisco, 84
Campos, Humberto de, 57
Carmelo, Antônio, 69
Carmelo, Jesuino do Monte, 23
Carvalho, Elysio de, 9, 16, 60–61
Carvalho, General Estévão Leitão de, 119
Carvalho, Ronald de, 61, 62
Castro, Fidel, 97, 98, 105
Celso, Afonso, 54–55, 64, 68, 76, 128
Ceylon, 98
China, 95, 98, 122
Christie, William D., 35–36
Cisplatine War, 36
Clémenceau, Georges, 53
Cleveland, Grover, 52
Coffee industry, 47, 51, 72, 77, 81, 95; and growth of influence of "coffee class," 48, 72–73, 74
Communist Party of Brazil (Partido Comunista Brasileiro), 75, 76, 90, 113, 120
Conselheiro, Antônio, 56
Constitutionalist Military Movement (Movimento Militar Constitucionalista), 117
Corção, Gustavo, 119–20
Correia, Raymundo, 54
Cosío Villegas, Daniel, 24
Costa, Francisco Augusto Pereira da, 58
Costa, Hipólito da, 34
Costa, Lúcio, 93

Coutinho, José Joaquim da Cunha de Azeredo, 25, 90–91
Couto, Domingos do Loreto, 22
Cuauhtémoc, 61–62
Cuba, 96, 97, 105, 107, 122
Cunha, Euclides da, 54, 55–56

Dantas, San Tiago, 98, 109, 110
Denis, King of Portugal, 4
Denis, Jean Ferdinand, 41
Dias, Gonçalves, 45
Dias, Henrique, 15
Dominican Republic, 122
Durão, José de Santa Rita, 22–23
Dutch, in Brazil, 13, 15, 16
Dutra, Eurico, 85, 87–88

Eletrobrás, 99, 101
Emboabas, War of the, 17
Escobar, Ildefonso, 86

Farquhar, Percival, 81
Fernandes, Hélio, 123
Ferreira, Alexandre Rodrigues, 23
Figueiredo, Jackson de, 70
Fonseca, Antônio José Vitorino Borges da, 22
Fonseca, Marshal Deodoro da, 49
Foreign policy, 16, 17–18, 27, 29 ff., 34–37, 47–48, 52–54, 94, 97–98, 121, 125, 126, 129
France, 13, 38, 46, 52
Franco, Afonso Arinos de Melo, 65
French Revolution, 4, 25
Freyre, Gilberto, 6, 43, 65
Furtado, Celso, 114

Gama, José Basílio da, 22
Gândavo, Pero de Magalhães de, 12
General Labor Command, 112
Germany, 52
Gilberto, João, 111
Gomes, Carlos, 45
Gomes, Eduardo, 67
Gomes, Lindolfo, 63
Gomes, Pimentel, 95
Goulart, João, 9, 90, 96, 97–100, 107, 108, 110, 112–14, 115, 117–18, 120, 129, 130

Grant, Andrew, 41
Great Britain, 13, 27, 30, 31, 34–36, 38, 105
Guevara, Ernesto Che, 97
Gusmão, Alexandre de, 18

Hague Peace Conferences, 53
Hanna Mining Corporation, 121
Holanda, Chico Buarque de, 106
Holanda, Sérgio Buarque de, 62, 65, 67

Inconfidências, 26
Indian Protection Service, 57
Indianist movement, 22, 44 ff., 57
Indians, 6, 8, 13, 15, 18, 19, 22, 39, 42, 44 ff., 55 ff., 65, 66
Industrialization, 52, 69, 77, 79–84, 86, 88, 93–94, 125, 129, 133
Institute of Social and Economic Studies (Instituto de Estudos Sociais e Econômicos), 110
Integralist party, 67, 75, 76, 90
Intellectuals, contributions to nationalism by, 9, 10, 14, 19–24, 25, 31, 39, 43 ff., 54–55, 56 ff., 60 ff., 85, 101–2, 106, 128, 133
Inter-American Peace Force, 122, 126
Interior: settlement of, 18, 19, 39, 55, 93, 119; as symbol, 5, 55, 56, 66; and "March to the West," 66, 86
International Monetary Fund, 93, 94, 123
Italy, 52, 115

Jaboatão, Antônio de Santa Maria, 21, 22
Jaguaribe, Hélio, 11, 24, 103
Japan, 112
Jefferson, Thomas, 26
Jequitinhonha, Visconde de, 44
Jesuits, 12–13, 20, 23, 70
João VI, King of Portugal, 29, 32, 79
Jobim, Antônio Carlos, 111
Johnson, Joseph Medupe, 96
Johnson, Lyndon B., 114, 115
Julião, Francisco, 107–8, 109

Kubitschek, Juscelino, 90, 92–94, 114, 117

Lacerda, Carlos, 116, 123, 126–27
Land reform, 105, 107–9, 118
Leme, Pedro Taques de Almeida Paes, 21
Levy, Alexandre, 45
Liberal Alliance, 73
Lima, Hermes, 9
Lima, Jorge de, 65
Lima Sobrinho, Barbosa, 7, 9, 37, 101
Lisboa, Antônio Francisco, 23
Lôbo, Edú, 111
Loiola, Inácio Bento de, 34
Lopes, João Simões, 63
López Mateos, Adolfo, 115
Lorillard, G. L., 72–73
Lott, Marshal Henrique Teixeira, 117–18, 124, 125
Luccock, John, 27–28
Luís, Washington, 74, 80

Madre de Deus, Gaspar da, 22
Madrid, Treaty of, 18
Magalhães, Benjamin Constant de, 49
Magalhães, Couto de, 57
Magalhães, Juracy, 121–22, 126
Magalhães, Sérgio, 110
Maía, José Joaquim, 26
Manaus, 52
Mann, Thomas C., 115
Manoel I, King of Portugal, 12
Mao Tse-tung, 97
Maranhão, 15, 19, 68
Martius, Karl Friedrich Philipp von, 41–43, 65
Mascates, War of the, 17, 32, 33
Matarazzo (family), 80
Mato Grosso, 18, 47
Matos, Gregório de, 16, 32
Maul, Carlos, 120
Meirelles, Vítor, 46
Melo Neto, João Cabral de, 106
Mendes, Sérgio, 111
Mendonça, Salvador de, 57
Mexico, 53, 83, 115

Military, 48–50, 75, 114 ff., 120 ff., 125 ff., 129–31, 132–33
Milliet, Sérgio, 67
Minas Gerais, 17, 18, 19, 23, 26, 33, 63, 72, 73
Mirales, José, 21, 22
Modern Art Week, 61, 63
Modernist movement, 61 ff., 66
Monteiro, Góes, 76
Moraes Filho, Alexandre José de Melo, 57, 58
Moreira, Neiva, 110
Morel, Edmar, 116
Mourão Filho, General Olímpio, 125

Napoleon I, 27
Napoleon III, 48
National Democratic Union (União Democrática Nacional), 94, 131
National Liberation Alliance (Aliança Nacional Libertadora), 75
National Liberation Front, 109
National Motor Industry (Fábrica Nacional de Motores), 121
National Parliamentary Front (Frente Parlamentar Nacionalista), 104, 105, 109–10
National Petroleum Council, 82
National Service of Historic and Artistic Patrimony, 85
National Social Action party (Ação Social Nacionalista), 68–69
National Student Union (União Nacional de Estudantes), 104–5, 121
National Telephone Company, 100
Nationalism: conservative, 36 ff., 69 ff., 74; cultural, 4, 6 ff., 9, 10, 19–20, 21, 23–24, 27, 39 ff., 43 ff., 60 ff., 69, 85, 111 ff., 128; definition of, 3–4, 9–10; developmental, 4–5, 8–9, 11, 16, 17, 102 ff., 128 ff.; economic, 11, 72 ff., 77–84, 86, 88, 89, 90–93, 94, 98 ff., 104 ff.; political, 9, 10–11, 24, 25, 26–28, 30, 50, 69, 76, 90
Nationality, formation of Brazilian, 4, 6–7, 17, 18–19, 42–43, 44 ff.
Nativism, 9, 14, 20, 24, 28, 30, 31, 40, 127, 128

Negroes, 15, 39, 42, 51, 56, 65, 96
Nepomuceno, Alberto, 45–46
Niemeyer, Oscar, 93, 114
Nigeria, 96

Oliveira, Jorge Marcos de, 124

Pacheco, Joaquim José, 37–38
Paraguay, 36, 47–48, 115
Pau-brasil, 66
Peace Corps, 100
Peasant Leagues, 107
Pedro I, Emperor of Brazil, 29–30, 32–33, 39, 47
Pedro II, Emperor of Brazil, 47, 48
Pelé, 111
Pereira, Nuno Marques, 20
Pereira, Temperani, 110
Pernambuco, 14, 15, 19, 22, 26, 67, 108
Peru, 53
Petrobrás, 83, 103, 105, 109, 110, 118, 121
Petroleum, 82, 126
Philip II, King of Spain, 15
Picchia, Minotti del, 60, 62, 67
Pinto, Alvaro Vieira, 103
Pinto, José de Magalhães, 126
Pita, Sebastião da Rocha, 20, 21, 40, 41
Pompeia, Raul, 43–44
Popular Mobilization Front, 109
Portugal, 4, 7, 9, 10, 13, 15 ff., 27, 29–30, 31 ff., 39, 46, 52, 70
Portuguese language, 5, 37, 57, 84
Prado, Eduardo, 91
Prado, Paulo, 64, 70
Prestes, Júlio, 68, 74
Prestes, Luís Carlos, 75
Principe, Hermógenes, 124

Quadros, Jânio, 90, 94, 95–97, 101, 114

Races, amalgamation of, 6, 8, 15, 16, 18–19, 42–43, 44 ff., 65, 95
Ramos, Graciliano, 111
Ramos, Nerêu, 84
Rangel, Alberto, 57

Recife, 17, 19, 33–34, 39, 75
Regionalism, 70–71, 73
Rêgo, José Lins do, 65, 111–12
Republican Party, 48
Ribeiro, João, 23
Ricardo, Cassiano, 66, 67, 80
Rio-Branco, Baron of, 52–53, 54, 97, 98, 126, 129
Rio de Janeiro, 15, 19, 27, 35–36, 39, 43, 49, 52, 53, 68, 72, 73, 75, 105, 113
Rio de la Plata, 10, 36, 47
Rio Grande do Sul, 35, 47, 67, 68, 73–74, 100
Rodrigues, João Barbosa, 57
Rodrigues, José Honório, 7, 55, 101
Roman Catholic Church, 5, 44, 48, 69–70, 76
Romero, Sílvio, 23, 24, 46, 58
Rondon, Cândido, 57
Root, Elihu, 53, 72
Rosa, Guimarães, 112
Rosas, Juan Manuel, 36

Salgado, Plínio, 65, 66, 67, 76, 120
Salles, Manuel Ferraz de Campos, 72
Salvador, Vicente do, 14, 21
Santos, 14, 52
Santos, John F., 6
São Francisco river, 15
São Leopoldo, Visconde de, 40–41
São Paulo, 15, 19, 20, 23, 52, 61, 68, 72, 73, 75, 80
Sardinha, Antônio, 67
Silva, José Bonifácio de Andrade e, 29, 39
Silva, Marshal Artur da Costa e, 125–26
Social Democratic Party (Partido Social Democrático), 87, 131
Society for the Nationalization of Commerce, 34
Sodré, Nelson Werneck, 11, 103
Sousa, Pero Lopes de, 12
Southey, Robert, 41
Soviet Union, 98
Spain, 15, 17–18, 25, 52
Spanish America, 5, 10, 18, 25, 31, 35 ff., 47, 79, 91, 98, 107, 117, 130, 131
Stroessner, General Alfredo, 115
Students, 101, 103, 104–5, 106, 126–27
Sugar industry, 13, 19, 47, 48, 51
Superintendency of the Development of the Northeast (Superintendência do Desenvolvimento do Nordeste), 93
Superior Institute of Brazilian Studies (Instituto Superior de Estudos Brasileiros), 102, 103–4, 121
Superior War College (Escola Superior de Guerra), 120

Tarso, Paulo de, 110
Taunay, Afonso de, 55
Tordesillas, Treaty of, 17
Tôrres, Alberto, 78–79, 91
Toynbee, Arnold, 133
Triple Alliance, War of the, 36, 47–48, 130
Turner, Frederick Jackson, 55

United Nations, 94, 122
United States, 30, 53, 96, 97, 98, 99–100, 112, 126; anti-Americanism, 91, 105, 108, 114–16, 120, 121, 123, 127
Urbanization Company of the New Capital (Companhia Urbanizadora da Nova Capital), 93
Uruguay, 36, 113

Vargas, Getúlio, 9, 11, 67, 74–75, 76–77, 79 ff., 82–89, 97, 102, 104, 107, 120, 129, 131, 133
Varnhagen, Francisco Adolfo de, 45
Vasconcellos, Manoel Meira de, 95
Vasconcelos, José, 61
Veloso, José Mariano da Conceição, 23
Verdamarelo, 66
Veríssimo, Erico, 112
Vidal, André, 15
Vieira, João Fernandes, 15
Viet-Nam, 122
Villa-Lobos, Heitor, 61, 111

Walters, General Vernon A., 115–16

Women's Republican Party (Partido Republicano Feminino), 57
World War I, 68
World War II, 80, 91, 93, 94, 104, 115

Xenophobia, 31 ff., 35 ff., 39 ff., 77, 79, 80, 90–91, 125, 128

Ypiranga river, 29